■ The Unanticipated City

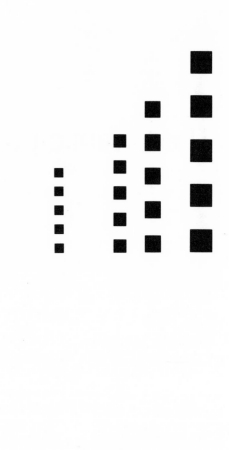

The Unanticipated City

Loft Conversions in Lower Manhattan

James R. Hudson

The University of Massachusetts Press

Amherst

1987

Copyright © 1987 by
The University of Massachusetts Press
All rights reserved
Printed in the United States of America
Designed by Barbara Werden
Set in Linoterm Trump Medieval at
The University of Massachusetts Press
Library of Congress Cataloging-in-Publication Data

Hudson, James R., 1933–
  The unanticipated city.

  Bibliography: p.
  Includes index.
    1. Urban renewal—New York (N.Y.) 2. Lofts—
New York (N.Y.) 3. SoHo (New York, N.Y.)
4. Manhattan (New York, N.Y.) I. Title.
HT177.N5H82   1988   307.3′36   87–6003
ISBN 0-87023-579-6 (alk. paper)

British Library Cataloging in Publication data are available

To the memory of H.S. and C.B.T.L.

Contents

Preface

When our older cities dominated the economic life of our nation, we tended, with few exceptions, to ignore their importance to our national culture. Their emphasis on profit and productivity seemed to overshadow their contributions to tradition, refinement, and humanitarian concerns. We believed that the influence of the urban environment upon individuals made them, at best, shrewd, self-aggrandizing, and exploitive of others, and, at worst, corrupt or psychotic. When we wished to epitomize our ideal national character, we turned to the small towns, rural areas, and the "frontier" for values and life-styles that we esteemed and cherished.

Now that the industrial significance of our cities has declined, we seem to have developed a certain nostalgia for our urban past: a nostalgia that has prompted us to reevaluate our cities' contributions to our heritage and culture, and even to discover desirable characteristics manifested by those who dwelt in them. These newly recognized contributions of our older urban environments are not restricted to the monuments, museums, and historical districts that we are now coming to truly appreciate. They are also to be found in the appeal of the quality of life inherent in the daily round of activities. Thus our new appreciation for our urban heritage not only has led us to find our older cities particularly appropriate as sites for national celebrations, but also has prompted many of us to consider these cities as good places in which to live and work.

Although we have carelessly destroyed some of their architectural achievements and let others decay or be grotesquely "modernized," the physical and cultural heritage of these cities has had and continues to have an important effect upon their growth and development, through both planning and "natural" cultural evolution. Each city has its own culture and heritage, products of its particular history. Therefore, unique heritage and culture must be addressed in any systematic study of the processes that have produced the social structure and social organization of each individual city.

This is not to deny that there are general processes that can be identified as affecting all our cities in similar ways, but to emphasize the central point that each city's individual characteristics—cultural, sociopolitical, geographical—produce unique configurations of those processes in any particular city at any given period. Therefore, unless an understanding of these unique individual characteristics is a part of general analysis, the analysis will be inexact and incomplete, and its use for retrospective interpretation and practical application in planning and guiding the future evolution of our cities will be seriously impaired.

When the key functions of these older cities were based upon the manufacture of goods—automobiles, steel, machine tools, and the host of consumer products produced by heavy industries—their tempo, rhythm, and organization revealed the hegemony of those industries. The exportation of the finished products to national and international markets and the importation of the raw materials needed for their production was reflected in the significance of their rail and port facilities. Now that the heavy industries that used these facilities have departed, new uses for rail centers and harbors are being found that indicate the fundamental changes in the economies of these cities. Some of us, like myself, who remember the Cuyahoga River in Cleveland as so polluted as to constitute a fire hazard, are stunned to see pleasure boats plying its waters, and new, high-rise apartment buildings on its banks. We are startled at this and other changes because we did not anticipate that these older cities had a promising future. We were worried about the mounting concentration of the poor and the elderly in their populations, their declining industrial bases, their decaying infrastructures, and their neglect by the federal government. When we see these promising changes, we wonder how they happened, why they happened, and what they indicate about the future of these cities. Where are these trends leading, and what is their significance for these cities and for our urban society in general? Such questions are addressed in this study, and the answers, while focused on a particular example, suggest clues about the more general directions of contemporary American society.

This study analyzes some of the elements of these trends in one area of New York City: the loft areas of Lower Manhattan. In one brief time span (1961–85), artists, converting old factories to residential/work spaces, transformed this area into a new, vital, productive community, despite numerous economic, political, bureaucratic, and cultural impediments. The study reveals that shrewd and combative character attributed to New Yorkers, who always seem to find niches for themselves in a rapidly changing environment where being quick-witted, fast-moving, and intensely alert are requirements for survival. It demonstrates how the cultural "ecosystem" of New York continues to offer opportunities for new and creative talent that must find suitable space in which to live and work. The study focuses on how the city accommodated to the unanticipated changes which these artists initiated and which fundamentally affected the planning of its future growth and development; it describes also how the city incorporated these changes into its own continuing attempts to meet and adjust to the challenge of new social conditions.

The study illustrates a pattern that is becoming increasingly common in our postindustrial cities, a pattern that combines a residential life-style, a special kind of production, and a form of urban entertainment into a new urban milieu that recognizes their industrial and commercial heritage as an era that has passed. The realization of this new pattern may have different expressions in different cities. The specialized industries in Pittsburgh, Cleveland, Akron, Detroit, Buffalo, Philadelphia, Baltimore, and New York gave the patterns associated with industry and commerce in each of these cities distinguishing features, yet despite these differences, the common elements of these patterns could be identified and analyzed. As the postindustrial patterns in these and other urban areas develop and reach maturity, new commonalities will become recognizable and lend themselves to generalizable comparisons. One of the major objectives of this study is to provide a basis upon which to build a general perspective for studying the postindustrial city.

Many urban sociologists recognize the substantial contribution that human ecological theory has made to the study of urban social organization by providing a holistic approach to analyzing the structure and functions of cities and patterns of urban growth. This contribution, however, is currently viewed by many urban researchers as historically important but theoretically flawed, and obviously outmoded. For many, human ecological theory has lost its analytic and interpretative powers to newer theoretical approaches.

One of the reasons for this attitude is that some of the initial formulations of human ecological theory were too closely tied to biological ecology and deterministic economic models. These approaches failed to give sufficient place to the effects of conscious social action by individuals and groups on social systems. Although these early theoretical problems have been overcome, the reputation based on these earlier oversights has persisted. Some current urban analysts eschew the human ecological approach because they perceive the findings of the early ecologists as representing the substance of the refined theory, rather than the results of its inexact application to a particular historical period. When these findings proved inaccurate under changing conditions, the theoretical principles were discarded along with the dated findings. The unfortunate identification of ecological theory itself with its early research applications obscures the refined theory's validity for analyzing contemporary social systems.

One objective of this study, then, is to demonstrate the continued validity and broad application of human ecological theory, building upon its traditional formulation (which remains essentially viable) and incorporating new theoretical conceptualizations that free it from some of its earlier limitations. In particular, this study emphasizes the importance of both local culture and conscious actions of individuals and groups in influencing land use patterns, and illustrates that these elements not only can, but must, be readily fitted into human ecological theory.

Thus in this study a refined and updated human ecological theory provides the analytic framework for examining the changing land use patterns of New York City's Lower Manhattan over the past thirty years—patterns that may well provide important clues to our understanding of emerging trends in the postindustrial development of our older cities throughout the United States. This approach should be useful in assisting us to appreciate, preserve, and celebrate our diverse urban culture—and in suggesting strategies based on the principles of urban social organization for dealing with some of the complicated issues in our dynamic contemporary social system.

Acknowledgments

This research would never have been begun if it had not been for an invitation from Professor Melvin Reichler in the spring of 1977 to join him and a group of his students in investigating SoHo. My work with Professor Reichler and his generous hospitality during my initial field work were invaluable to this study.

Members of various agencies in New York City were also helpful to that first summer of research. Anne Pizzicarra and Sandy Hornick provided a good deal of the data that I have used in the analysis. In 1979, Lancelot Fletcher asked me to participate in research under the direction of Ira Brophy at the Office of Economic Development on the impact of residential conversions of industrial lofts on the city's economy. I was given access to all the data gathered in that research project for my own work. In addition, under the auspices of that office I was able to gain the cooperation of several other agencies in New York City that were investigating the changes occurring in Lower Manhattan.

Others who have done research on loft conversions shared, in various degrees, their data, results, and insights: James Ballinson, Kristina Ford, Charles R. Simpson, and Sharon Zukin. I have made good use of their findings, as noted in the text.

Scott Riddle housed me during the field work in 1980 and 1981. Not only was he a good host, but his willingness to walk the streets of Lower Manhattan with me and his knowledge of the city were constant sources of help. Grace Fisher and Monty Wasch have often let me bed down in their loft, and their contacts in the city proved to be an invaluable resource for this research.

Stanley N. Miller juggled my academic schedule in ways that permitted me to commute to New York City to do the field work while maintaining my normal academic responsibilities. Herb Hunter, Rie Gentlzer, Clem Gilpin, Bob Colman, and Simon Bronner were very supportive colleagues not only in offering comments and insights on the research, but also in carrying an extra share of the burden of our program during my absences in the field.

Charles Jackson, Brady Stroh, and Robert F. Munzenrider worked with me preparing my data for machine tabulation and solving some methodological problems. The staff of the Heindel Library at Capital College assisted me continuously in my search for the various materials that I needed for this work.

Gerald D. Suttles did an extraordinary amount of work on early drafts of this manuscript, and helped shape my final approach to the research problem. Robert B. Wolf worked constantly to turn my leaden writing into readable prose, and enhanced the clarity and logic of my analysis by his demanding standards.

Kathy Ritter, Louisa Morgan, and Daria Sessamen typed endless drafts and demonstrated a degree of patience that can only be fully appreciated by those who have had the pleasure of working with them.

Finally, Maureen Powers made my work easier by her tolerance for someone obsessed with inner city redevelopment and a little bit compulsive about research, and by sharing with me the joys of parenting her delightful and stimulating sons, Matthew and Ethan.

■ The Unanticipated City

1 ■ Human Ecology: Tool for Urban Analysis

The Problem: Analyzing Contemporary Urban Social Change

Since they first emerged as one form of human organization, cities have stimulated inquiring minds to consider their structure, organization, and social consequences. With the development of modern social science, speculation on these topics has been replaced with more systematic and scientific research. Whether this research has concentrated on urban expansion or contraction, prosperity or decay, mental health or pathology, increase or decline in the number of cities in any social system, it has focused on one overriding concern—the causes and consequences of urban social change. The following investigation of the conversion of commercial and industrial buildings to residential use in New York City over the past twenty-five years offers data and analysis which I hope contribute significantly to effectively addressing that concern.

The conversion of old industrial and commercial buildings to residential and new retail uses has been going on in the United States for a number of years. In most cases it has occurred on such a limited scale that it might be regarded as an ecological sport—so limited that it could be taken as the exception proving the traditional rule that the more intense usages of commerce and industry crowd out those of residence and craft activities. Large-scale altera-

3

tion of this accepted pattern, such as the residential conversion in Lower Manhattan—particularly in the areas now known as SoHo, NoHo, and TriBeCa—challenges this rule and clearly requires more complete explanation than that usually found in studies of changes in land use patterns.

In order to begin to perceive the significance of this example of residential conversion, it will be useful to review some general trends that have altered the social organization of American society since the end of World War II. One of the major shifts has been the redistribution of population, commerce, and industry from the centers of cities to the suburbs, and from the northeastern and midwestern to the sunbelt states. Housing policies of the federal government, such as tax breaks and insured loans, have facilitated the movement of the middle classes into the suburbs. The development of a vast interstate road system has assisted this redistribution of population and manufacturing and commercial concerns. The dominant economic activities in the United States have shifted from extraction and fabrication to service and knowledge industries, and this shift has abetted the changes recorded by urban economists and sociologists.

Such changes have contributed to the decline and decay of our older cities: the incidence of social disorganization, however measured, has its highest rates in these older cities. Such cities—Boston, Detroit, Baltimore, Philadelphia—are often the subjects of media commentary on what is wrong with the current economy. Unemployment statistics are always grimmest in such cities, where buildings are abandoned, arson becomes a means of profit, and people drop out of the occupational structure, even disappear from the relief system. Yet when realized potentials for urban revitalization and rejuvenation are sought, these same cities become spotlighted examples. Boston's harbor areas, Detroit's Renaissance Center, Baltimore's Inner Harbor, Philadelphia's Society Hill—all have been featured as examples of how older cities can be salvaged and given new life.

Such features as the recycling of old commercial and industrial buildings are often highlighted as indicators of the future economic promise of older cities. A recycled tobacco warehouse in

Richmond; a department store in Lancaster, Pennsylvania; a printing plant in Philadelphia; grain silos in Akron, Ohio; a torpedo factory in Alexandria, Virginia; and a chocolate factory in San Francisco are newsworthy examples of an extensive movement toward using existing structures for new purposes—purposes that their developers and the administrators of the cities hope will restore vitality and stem the course of urban decay and deterioration.

There is also a growing body of literature on the process of restoration and renovation of older housing stock (Laska and Spain, 1980; *Urban Affairs Quarterly*, June 1980; Stratton, 1977). City after city is shown to have some older neighborhoods that have suffered from neglect which are now being transformed into middle-class and upper middle-class enclaves. The discovery of our architectural history has given impetus to the restoration of Georgian, Federal, and Victorian homes to their original splendor or, in extreme cases, "to their original inconveniences" (Suttles, 1979:7). It is not yet possible to assess the impact of these activities on the overall social organization of older cities, but the evidence clearly indicates that there are a number of middle-class households who find the inner cities attractive and are willing to make investments in revitalizing these neighborhoods. The suburbs are no longer the only destination for the upwardly mobile middle class. The appeal of the suburban way of life does not seem to have waned for households with two or more children, but among the growing number of households with two incomes and one or no children, urban residence has won increasing adherents.

This population, popularly known as "yuppies," has chosen locations near the center of cities, close to their work places, within easy reach of those cultural and recreational facilities enjoyed by the more affluent and highly educated. Although our attention has been drawn primarily to these more affluent new urban residents, there have been other householders who have also found the inner cities attractive. A growing number of single parent households, particularly those headed by females, are discovering that inner city housing is more affordable than that in the suburbs. Their need for readily accessible child care and convenient household maintenance services has made urban residence appealing.

The same is true for those occupational groups that are finding jobs in the lower skilled positions of the new urban entertainment zones.

The generally accepted term for the process of restoration/renovation of urban neighborhoods by middle-class households is gentrification or, more aptly, "urban reinvasion" (London, 1980:77). But what has been happening in Lower Manhattan does not fit exactly into this category, since the converted buildings had no previous use as residences, and their architecture, while interesting to industrial designers and urban historians, is hardly Victorian, Georgian, or Federal. The neighborhood revitalization literature concentrates on units used continuously as residential dwellings, and places some importance on ambience and style. The generalizations on gentrification have some application to Lower Manhattan, but primarily in terms of the population that has moved in, not the types of areas in which this process has occurred.[1]

Just how exceptional have the residential conversions of manufacturing and commercial buildings in SoHo, NoHo, TriBeCa, and other areas of Lower Manhattan been? Do they seriously challenge long-standing propositions about changing land usage, the value of central location, and accessibility? Are the rumors and reports of political and economic manipulation only a mythologized explanation of the working of some "ecological force," or have politicians, developers, artists, and yuppies played an active part in this reconstruction of New York's urban landscape? If the latter is the case, how can the activities of these social actors be incorporated into an explanation of contemporary urban social organization, adaptation, and change? Further, do these changes portend some trend toward fundamental future alteration in the development of our older postindustrial cities, not simply an occasional haphazard recycling of deteriorated areas carried out by a small cadre of young urban professionals who find some areas of these cities attractive? Are we witnessing an unanticipated major change in the course of the development of our cities that urban planners, sociologists, and politicians have yet to identify and address effectively? The validity of any sociological theory as an interpreter and to some extent a predictor of urban social change rests on its ability to provide answers to these questions.

The Analytic Approach: Ecological Theory Refined

The major organizing theoretical framework for this analysis is human ecology—more particularly, the ecological theory developed by Amos H. Hawley and others over the past forty years. In addition, I have relied to some extent on the work of urban economists, urban geographers, and other urban sociologists who have provided me with useful insights into the patterns of urban form and change. I have also included some elements from the theories of political sociology and community organization in developing my perspective.[2]

Human ecology offers a holistic approach to studying social change; it places great emphasis on the environment in which social systems operate. Whether natural or man-made, environment "is seen as presenting the problem of life and as providing a means for its resolution" (Hawley, 1968:330). The social organizaton of any system is regarded as the product of the interaction between population and environment. In ecological theory, environment is neither static nor deterministic, but rather a changing set of limiting conditions to which a population adapts. Alterations in the environment, however they may occur, pose an ongoing challenge to social systems, and successful adaptations must be made to new environmental conditions if any social system is to survive. The degree of change and the form of adaptation, of course, varies with the specific problems that alterations in environment create at any particular time.

Using this general paradigm, human ecology has provided a useful framework for conceptualizing the process by which cities grow or decline, develop patterns of land use, and organize relationships with other parts of the social system, including other cities. Although often attacked by its critics and misused by its practitioners, ecological theory nonetheless continues to be a rich source of concepts and hypotheses that can be used effectively to study and explain urban structure and, in particular, urban social change.

Human ecological theory, like any good theory, has been modified and refined through careful incorporation of new empirical evidence. Hawley reformulated earlier ecological theory to eliminate some of its unwarranted assumptions and inappropriate biological analogies (1944; 1950; 1968). He refined the theory to direct attention to what he considered to be the pivotal issue for ecological investigation—the "form and development" of human social systems. He conceptualized these social systems as characteristic of any population that develops social organization. His emphasis is on the social system as a whole and on its organized parts, not upon its individual members.

According to Hawley, a population's social organization is its mechanism for adapting to its environment. In ecological theory, environment is defined as whatever is external to the system under study; it has no fixed content. No matter how specifically defined, an environment sets limits on the social system, but does not wholly, or even necessarily, determine its form or development. Hawley recognizes that people can modify and alter the environment through inventions, the use of tools, complex social arrangements, and other strategies which mitigate the environment's impact on the system. Yet no matter how extensive these modifications or alterations, the environment impinges on the population. Environment does not change to "assist" social systems, but must be accepted as something that demands adjustment on the part of the social system itself. Such adjustment emphasizes "man's great facility for devising and accumulating methods of coping with life situations," which "is evidence of a dynamics of human behavior that is without counterpart elsewhere in the animate world" (Hawley, 1950:68–69). This unique attribute of humans is what makes possible a human ecology "distict from a general ecology" (Hawley, 1950:69).

Hawley's reformulation of ecological theory has led him to reexamine the priority early human ecologists gave some concepts, particularly competition. Until Hawley, many human ecologists had reached their most complete agreement with urban economists and geographers in regarding competition as perhaps the most important factor in the allocation of land use. Hurd's early formulation of the concept of competition (1903) served as a guide to succeeding generations of urban land use analysts. His first general principle was: "Since value depends on economic rent, and rent on location, and location on convenience, and convenience on nearness, we may eliminate the intermediate steps and say that value depends upon nearness" (1970:13). The idea contained in this statement has been developed into the concept of "friction of space" employed by human ecologists to analyze the spatial distribution of economic and social activities. Hurd contended that the most successful activities in the bidding for land are commercial and industrial businesses. He laid out the general principle that in the competition over land, "residences are early driven to the circumference, while business remains in the centre, and as residents divide into social grades, retail shops of corresponding grades follow the residences, and wholesale shops in turn follow the retailers, while institutions and various mixed utilities irregularly fill in the intermediate zone, and the banking and office section remains as the main business centre" (1970:15). Those familiar with subsequent theory and research can discern the embryonic concepts of the concentric zonal hypothesis, clustering, succession, invasion, and the Central Business District within Hurd's formulation.

Hurd distinguished sharply between the major factors determining land use for business and land use for residence. He maintained that the distribution of all business activities depends purely on economic forces, with "land going to the highest bidder and the highest bidder being the one who made land earn the largest amount" (1970:77). Thus the "basis of residence values is social and not economic—even though land goes to the highest bidder— the rich selecting the locations which please them, those of moderate means living as near as possible, and so on down the scale of wealth" (1970:77–78). Hurd also indicated an additional differentiation between the factors governing residential and commercial land use, maintaining that "business property is selected by the man from an economic standpoint, and residence by the woman from a social standpoint" (1970:78). Urban land values and land use distribution, therefore, are determined by factors operating on two different levels: the economic level, which reflects market mechanisms; and the social-psychological level, which reflects personal values.

But creating an arbitrary distinction between economic and social values to explain commercial and residential land use patterns has proven to be ineffective in explaining those patterns. Simple economics cannot explain the decisions of some business firms to build architecturally distinguished buildings. For example, Toll describes the values incorporated into the Woolworth and Equitable buildings at the turn of the century: "Their architecture and the circumstances in which they were made embodied the cult of the self-made man, and the glittering religion of wealth and success, the energies of industrialism, and the lawlessness out of which many early twentieth-century American cities fashioned their inner hearts" (1969:55–57). The same symbolic values were, no doubt, part of the reasons for the design of the Lever House and Seagram Building six decades later.[3]

Obviously, urban land may be more or less appropriate for different uses. Some locations may offer a very limited scope of potential use. Hurd argued that when land has a limited utility, "its value is proportionate to the degree to which it serves that purpose and the amount which such utility can afford to pay for it" (1970:145). When there are competing purposes, "one utility competes against another and the land goes to the highest utilization" (1970:145). Implicit in this argument is the contention that the changing social organization of a city can create a new set of "utilities," and therefore a concomitant potential for alteration of land use patterns.[4] The conversion of commercial and industrial spaces to residential use exemplifies such an alteration. On the face of it, this change does not fit Hurd's zonal model; however, a reasonable argument can be made that a new "utility" did facilitate change in Lower Manhattan, but for reasons Hurd did not recognize in his theory.

According to Hurd, then, the primary force determining the distribution of businesses and residents into their spatial patterns was

economic. Orderly spatial patterns are a consistent finding in ecological research; but attributing such patterns solely to economic
competition results in a simplistic and erroneous explanation of
the development of urban land use patterns. Critics of ecological
theory (see, for example, Hollingshead, 1947; Bernard, 1973; Willhelm, 1962; and Zeitz, 1979) persist in pinning this crude formulation on contemporary human ecology. Hawley has cautioned
us against giving it the dominant position it had in early ecological thought. The "competitive hypothesis," as he notes, "is a
gross oversimplification of what is involved in the development
of pattern, structure, or other manifestations of organization"
(1944:401). Furthermore, "competition is not the pivotal concep-
tion of ecology; in fact, it is possible to describe the subject without
even an allusion to competition" (1944:401). Competition remains an important concept in ecological theory, but rather than
the sole cause of "fundamental differentiation and organization,"
it must be seen as "one among several influential factors" (Hawley, 1950:204). In contemporary ecological theory, social systems
are not solely determined by either economic or environmental
factors: a broader explanatory perspective than early ecological
theorists proposed is required to understand the patterns of social
organization, including land use.

In economics and ecology, competition has often been linked
with the concepts of intensity and density, which have an equally
important explanatory role. Intensity refers to the amount or frequency of activities at a given location, as examplified by intensive
farming, or the around-the-clock activities in a hospital emergency
room. The concept of intensity, then, can refer either to a highly
specialized use in a relatively restricted area or to a complex division of labor tightly organized in a relatively small space.

Density measures the number of different activities (or uses)
found in a given location such as a Central Business District,
which usually contains a wide range of businesses, services, and
people crowded together, often in high-rise buildings. When applied to housing, density is indicated by the number of persons per
room or the number of dwelling units per some spatial dimension.

Competition for space can add to land values; businesses will
pay for desirable locations, households will bid up the prices of

homes in "good" neighborhoods, and locations that become socially defined as prestigious can influence the market for both
businesses and households within them. The ways in which the
market value shifts vary because of a large number of factors. In
this study, a survey of the change in the market values of loft
spaces and buildings in Lower Manhattan will illustrate one pattern of this process. A description of the relations among competition, density, and intensity will demonstrate how their reciprocal
influences operated to raise rents and prices in the areas under
study.

The concepts of competition, density, and intensity form the
conceptual foundation on which a good deal of urban land use
theory rests. Much effort has gone into mitigating the connota-
tions of economic determinism inherent in these terms. The
effects of zoning (Willhelm, 1962), racial animosity (Duncan and
Duncan, 1957), and ethnic solidarity (Firey, 1947) have all been
posited as intervening variables explaining seeming exceptions to
the patterns that a crude economic model dictates or a simplistic
ecological explanation provides. These efforts, however, have not
eliminated the importance of these concepts in land use theory;
nor have empirical findings produced any new generalizatons with
equal usefulness. As an initial working proposition, nothing has
replaced the fundamental principle that competition among businesses, households, and individuals is a major influence in shaping
land use patterns. The ability of some to outbid others in the
marketplace continues to influence the territorial division of labor
that can be found in cities.

This fundamental working proposition, however, is no longer
accepted uncritically. The simplistic models that the first ecologists proposed have been replaced with more sophisticated ones—
although there are those who persist in criticizing contemporary
ecological theory on the basis of these earlier models. It is now
taken as axiomatic among ecologists, as well as among other social
scientists, that knowledge about how a social system works makes
it possible to anticipate, and therefore modify, if not control, its
development—within some broad limits. Ecologists have now
recognized that even their own research on social systems affects

the decisions that groups and individuals make in their attempts to control the development of their society. As Berry and Kasarda conclude, "The most important social change of our time is the spread of awareness that we have the ability to strive and deliberately to contrive change itself" (1977:429). What human actors will do and what the consequences of their actions will be can never be perfectly predicted (Merton, 1936). But that more rational actions producing more predictable results are possible through the use of social science is clearly evident.

Ordinarily, commercial and industrial interests have a competitive edge over residential populations in acquiring accessible locations because of their ability to outbid them in the marketplace. Similarly, financially able businesses can outbid others for advantageous sites. Social actions can modify market mechanisms. Zoning is an obvious example, even though zoning is often a method that also can be used to protect investments and assist in economic development. It can insure market values and stabilize land use patterns to promote an economic system over time.

New York City had the first zoning regulations, passed in 1916 under pressure from prosperous merchants with stores on Fifth Avenue. The Fifth Avenue Association wanted to stop the invasion of *manufacturing loft buildings* that were threatening to displace these stores and ruin the ambience of the streets for their customers. "What was coming up the avenue in hot pursuit was the garment industry. It sought the same thing as the carriage trade merchant—gain—but its route was lower Fifth Avenue, its great weapon was the tall loft building, its generals were real estate speculators, and its troops were lower East Side immigrants" (Toll, 1969:110). The first set of zoning regulations stayed this invasion, forcing the garment district westward to its present location, and stabilizing the loft buildings areas below Fourteenth Street.

As this earlier example indicates, then, the market is not beyond the influence or control of human actors. In addition to zoning, other mechanisms operate to modify its operation. Firey (1947) has pointed out that some land, like the Boston Common, may be protected because of its great symbolic importance. (But as Hawley [1947] noted in his review of Firey's study, the adjacent lands increased in value because of this action.) Some residents are willing to pay a premium for certain locations. Such a premium may not make economic "sense," but it nevertheless affects land use patterns.

Much of the literature on modern urban social organization has emphasized the population's preference for separation of work place and residence (Janowitz, 1978:264–319). Changes in the social organization of households and families, however, may be altering this preference. For instance, the number of single-headed families, childless couples, and unmarried adults organized as households has increased, and these households seem likely to allocate space in their homes differently from more traditional families. In addition, they require services to meet their household needs. Finally, they can introduce new social norms—all of which can modify existing residential patterns.

The presence of these new types of households indicates a logical need to reexamine the accepted patterns of urban growth and development. Although it appears in many forms and with many modifications, such growth and development is usually thought to proceed from the center outward.[5] Burgess's concentric zonal hypothesis (1925) is probably the best known formulation of this theory, but Hoyt's (1939) sector hypothesis also includes centripetal urban expansion. Burgess's paradigm posits the increasing size of the Central Business District replacing other land uses at its rim, thus setting off a sequence of movements outward. The more marginal businesses displace residents, and the displaced residents move further from the center. The accepted pattern suggests that social class is the variable that determines how far from the center a given household will move—the poorest nearest the center, the more prosperous at the perimeter, with gradients of the remaining households between the two.

No matter if one uses Burgess or Hoyt to study urban growth, two elements are consistent. The first is that changing land use patterns are initiated from the center of the city: it is the growth of the Central Business District that triggers subsequent alterations in land use patterns. The second is that the residential movement follows a gradient pattern correlated with household income. Because of their more intensive and profitable use of land, commerce and industry replace residential use. Residential land use may, moreover, go through phases of increasing density (e.g., from single household use, to boarding house to multihousehold use, to apartment dwelling use).

The method by which the Central Business District theoretically expands is an illustration of a process described in ecological theory as "invasion-succession," the two terms of which are often linked but refer to separate processes. "Invasion" refers to the entrance of a new population into an area that is either pristine or already occupied. "Succession" indicates the series of events or stages that occur as the new population increases in numbers and comes to dominate the area. These theoretical propositions are found in early ecological theory, and have been supported by a large body of empirical work (McKenzie, 1924, 1926; Park, 1936; Cressey, 1937; Hawley, 1950; Duncan and Duncan, 1957).

The ways in which the processes of invasion and succession are initiated vary widely. New technologies may enable a social system to expand, and that expansion may lead to the relocation of some activities and their replacement by others. More specifically, a transportation innovation can open new areas for residence, commerce, and industry. New patterns of land use replace older ones as succession continues. Population growth can generate pressures that spur migration—even if it is only to an adjacent neighborhood—and the new population can change the existing social organization by bringing with it new institutions, social customs, and a different demographic profile. Or a particular residential population can decline, thus opening housing for a different population—a common finding in studies of residential succession (Aldrich, 1975). Because of the variety of ways in which the process begins and the various results that can occur, ecological theory has not provided any standard predictive paradigms nor any necessary stages for its development (Duncan and Duncan, 1957:11–12). Human ecology only stipulates that the process is continuous everywhere, even though there may be varying periods of stability, some extensive.

Human ecological theory offers a strong conceptual framework for analyzing urban social change. But the current theory does have its limitations. Human ecological theory has not been stretched far enough to take into account all the dynamics of changes in land use patterns. Although it offers the most credible base for beginning such a study, additional perspectives are needed to provide a more complete picture. These other perspectives are included in this study to interpret the social dynamics that were at work in Lower Manhattan during the loft conversion movement of the last twenty-five years.

Application: Lower Manhattan, 1950s–1980s

The city's enormous size intensifies the complexity of analyzing urban social change within it, creating elaborate ramifications, combinations, and intricacies not found in smaller cities. The division of labor in its economic, social, and built environment exemplifies how elaborate the social organization of a city can be. Social change is not only ubiquitous in New York City, it occurs on a scale and in forms that prompt public attention. In New York, because they do things in a big way, what may go unnoticed elsewhere is exposed to national scrutiny. Other, smaller cities may frequently be the seats of innovation: it is the Big Apple, however, that legitimizes the new, the unique, and the dramatic. This is true whether it be nouvelle cuisine, clothing styles, or the conversion of commercial and industrial buildings to residential use.

Like other older cities, New York is beset with serious urban problems. The social collapse of the South Bronx has been vividly documented. Jane Jacobs (1961) used a New York neighborhood to illustrate how an urban society can deteriorate. The city's inability to stem this deterioration, despite concerted effort, demonstrated for Jacobs what she concluded were failures of public and private urban policies. The ineffectiveness of New York City in staving off its own decline has been pointed out over and over again by other urban analysts. In 1964, *Fortune* magazine published a cover story entitled "New York: A City Destroying Itself." The author emphasized political mismanagement, poor planning, and greed as the major causes of New York's decline. New York, the article maintained, had not made adequate provision for the changes in the needs of its population, the requirements of industry, and the structures of economic production. Without apparent intent, the magazine placed on the same page an advertisement that featured a 400,000-square-foot plant located in a parklike setting in South Carolina. The juxtaposition of this ad with the article describing the crush of rush hour traffic and the vanishing open spaces in New York City told its own story—and it was not entirely one of greed and corruption.

The interstate highway system has helped disperse commerce and industry throughout the nation. New York is linked to its immediate region by a system of limited access highways that have encouraged the exodus of its population and businesses. The interchanges along these highways are now nodes of commercial and industrial activities that were once housed in the boroughs of New York. The pattern is reminiscent of the earlier development of satellite business areas at junctures of the radial and circumferential streets within cities (Harris and Ullman, 1945), and it occurred for much the same reasons.

When one views New York City from the perspective of the mass media, in which the focus is on extremes—the glamour of the Upper East Side of Manhattan, or the urban blight of the South Bronx—one may fail to recall that, like other cities, it is a composite of hundreds of neighborhoods. A large proportion of residents of the city see themselves as living in one or another of these little worlds. There are, of course, all kinds of distinctions among these neighborhoods. Some, such as Chinatown and Little Italy, are not only the residences of special populations, but also tourist attractions because of their ethnic goods and ambience. Others, like the Hasidic enclaves, are less open, but represent distinct neighborhoods with residential populations who are loyal to local organizations, institutions, customs, and businesses. The presence and vitality of these neighborhoods support the observations of a number of urban researchers that large segments of urban dwellers want the social support of local neighborhoods and build institutions to sustain their local cultures (Fischer, 1976; Suttles, 1968; Hunter, 1974).

New York, then, is like a good many other large older cities with decaying infrastructures, declining urban amenities, shrinking numbers of manufacturing jobs, and aging, decaying housing stock. It is also like them in its areas of tremendous growth, increasing competition for office space, strong market for luxury housing, and expanding economy. In short, there is such an unevenness about New York that paradox and contradiction make any assessment of its future difficult. One way of generalizing about the city is to stress its decline; another is to highlight its areas of growth and recovery; still another is to see the present period as one of continuing transition, in a movement from the carefully documented city of the nineteenth century to the unanticipated one of the twentieth. The transition, like all changes, has not been and will not be painless or easy. Active intervention in planning and developing New York's future by government, private groups, and individuals will undoubtedly continue to affect this transition, for better and for worse.

Manhattan differs from the other boroughs in a number of ways, and since this study has its focus there, these differences need to be indicated. In the first place, Manhattan continues to have the largest concentration of manufacturing; thus, decreases in this sector of economic activity have an important impact there. In addition, Manhattan has the most expensive housing units, the highest densities of population, the most affluent and highly educated population, and the most competitive housing market of the five boroughs.

Manhattan shares with other boroughs of New York a number of discrete areas in which recent social changes have altered social organization and land use patterns. Some of the causes of these changes have already been suggested. The particular patterns of change depend upon a number of factors such as population, social institutions, location, economic activities, interest groups, and social actors. The recent changes in Lower Manhattan are a result of the operation of these factors in a particular area of New York; effective, detailed analysis of these changes provides the opportunity to expand the scope of human ecological theory's capacity to explain the processes influencing contemporary urban social organization, to identify trends, and to provide information that will guide social policy.

2 ■ Invasion-Succession in SoHo

The Process of Invasion-Succession, 1850–1960

SoHo is an acronym for the forty-three-block area in Manhattan south of Houston Street,[1] one of the communities defined by the New York City Bureau of Community Planning, and a zoning district (see fig. 1). Three of its boundaries are six-lane streets that separate it from contiguous areas—the type of separation frequently noted by those studying the inner city as giving neighborhoods unity and distinctness. The eastern boundary is not as clearly delineated, but the adjacent area on that side is Manhattan's Little Italy, and the neighborhood differences between buildings and land use are sharp enough to make a line of demarcation apparent. There are three streets in the northwest quadrant that have a high concentration of tenement structures and are considered to be part of Greenwich Village; these are not in the officially zoned district of SoHo. These streets, however, have been invaded by activities associated with SoHo's life-style and are usually included in popular descriptions of the area.

The series of changes through which this part of Lower Manhattan has passed can be effectively described by use of the ecological concept of invasion-succession. To review this concept: invasion is identified as that point at which a new population or land use enters an area or begins to develop; succession refers to "the series of events or stages involved in the replacement in an area of one

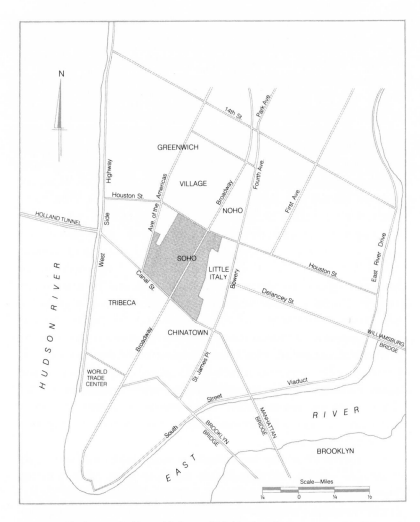

■ Lower Manhattan: SoHo and Adjacent Neighborhoods
(Courtesy Keith R. Gentzler)

type of occupant or land use by another" (Hawley, 1950:321). As the process matures, the area "settles into a fixed pattern which is resistant to pressures of change for a time, but eventually yields to a new type of occupant" or land use (Hawley, 1971:99).

The process often begins in response to changes in the larger system of which the area is a part, proceeds through several stages until a new balance or equilibrium is achieved, then begins again in response to a new set of conditions (Duncan and Duncan, 1957:133). The beginning of the process can be more readily identified than the subsequent stages, because any area in which the process occurs has usually been in equilibrium for some time. There are no established guidelines in ecological theory for identifying specific stages in the process, although there have been some suggested patterns offered (Aldrich, 1975; Hoover and Vernon, 1962; McKenzie, 1924). The usual method is to employ some heuristic device to identify stages (Duncan and Duncan, 1957: 11–12). The process may be under way before the preceding one has run its course (Hawley, 1950:402). Nor does the process have to reach the point at which there has been an entire replacement of the original population or establishment of totally new land use patterns. "The area may have a mixed population or land use patterns for a number of years" (Duncan and Duncan, 1957:109). These various components of invasion-succession are found throughout SoHo's history, including the period from 1955 to 1985 covered by this study.

In the middle of the nineteenth century, SoHo was one of the most fashionable neighborhoods in New York, with gracious houses and the best department stores, restaurants, and hotels.[2] Located within walking distance from what was then a major employment center downtown, it attracted high-income residents and the services such a population demands. This fashionable era lasted no more than twenty years, to about 1850. At that time, the middle-class population began to move toward midtown Manhattan, following the very wealthy, who were beginning to construct their palatial mansions along Fifth Avenue, first in the Thirties and then beyond the higher numbered cross streets. The increasing availability of streetcars, and later subways, enabled the prosperous to widen the distance between their workplaces and residences (Fischler, 1976).

In the next twenty years, this middle-class neighborhood deteriorated; at first, the stately homes became brothels, and later were cut into small apartments for the poor. The decaying housing stock was then replaced through the construction of new loft buildings beginning in 1879, providing space for mercantile and manufacturing businesses. Many of the buildings had prefabricated cast-iron parts, a unique innovation in building construction for that period (see Gayle and Gillon, 1974: "Introduction"). The design provided for large front and rear windows that illuminated the open floor space within. These buildings had (and have) a certain grandeur. As one observer commented, "One was supposed to walk down West Broadway to see the beauty of the renaissance, rewired in modern iron" (Koch, 1976:117). This architectural innovation was to provide one argument for saving the area from being razed, and was to become an important factor in public and private support for the new residential conversions begun in the 1960s (see Landmarks Preservation Commission, 1973).

From the middle of the 1870s until the beginning of World War I, SoHo and other areas of Lower Manhattan enjoyed economic prosperity as centers of manufacturing. Two major area industries were fabrication of women's and children's garments and the wholesale fur trade. These industries flourished, in part, because of the close proximity of an immigrant labor force housed in the Lower East Side, as well as because of the public and private transportation systems that permitted easy access by buyers and efficient shipment of the final products to local and national markets.

Just before World War I, as garment manufacturers, following retail outlets,[3] moved up Broadway toward the garment center's current location in the upper Thirties along Broadway and Seventh Avenue, the spaces vacated by these industries were filled by "a variety of establishments with a concentration of firms dealing with low value paper and textile wastes" (Rapkin, 1963:105). Two changes in transportation helped favor this alteration in land use patterns. The first was the 1904 opening of major subway lines that started at City Hall and moved up the West Side. This enabled the labor force housed in the Lower East Side to commute to work in the new factories in the garment district for a nickel each way. And when the Pennsylvania Railroad Station opened in 1912, it changed the buying and selling patterns of New York's garment center. Showrooms, entertainment facilities, and other marketing activities clustered in this midtown location. Easy access to railroad shipment facilities expedited the distribution of the final products to places outside New York. All of this pulled garment firms from other areas in Lower Manhattan to this emerging center of the trade.

Between 1920 and 1950 (with a small reprieve caused by the mobilization during World War II), SoHo declined significantly as a viable commercial and industrial area. To many, it began to be considered an anachronism in Manhattan's economy. It was known as Hell's Hundred Acres because of its demonstrated potential for major fires (Rapkin, 1963: 152–54). There were proposals for razing its buildings and constructing middle-income housing. The arguments put forward for rebuilding SoHo reflected the plans for the future of Lower Manhattan that called for developing it as a center of international commerce. The new office construction, such as the World Trade Center, planned and already under way, would create a market for middle- and upper-income housing in the area.

Thus, by the late 1950s, SoHo had become part of a larger area described by the ecological concept "zone of transition" (Griffin and Preston, 1966). Most of its businesses were marginal at best, or so it appeared. Some buildings had only a few tenants, others were boarded up, and still others had been razed and replaced by parking lots. A number of its building spaces were occasionally used for a variety of temporary activities, such as selling distressed merchandise or seasonal goods like Christmas decorations.

During this period there was vigorous development just beyond SoHo's boundaries. On the north, New York University was playing a key role by developing its campus, replacing loft buildings with apartment housing. Greenwich Village, never dormant, spread eastward and westward, creating new centers of entertainment and housing catering to hippies, yippies, and assorted bo-

■ The E. V. Haughwout Building built in 1857 stands on the corner of Broome and Broadway in the heart of SoHo. Its cast-iron facade is executed in the manner of the Venetian Renaissance. Haughwout specialized in selling cut-glass, silverware, clocks, and chandeliers. (Photo courtesy of the New York Landmarks Preservation Commission.)

■ Built in 1873, this five-story building with a cast-iron facade was designed as a warehouse. It is probably the best example of the French Second Empire style in SoHo. (Photo courtesy of the New York Landmarks Preservation Commission.)

hemians—as well as to traditional middle-class households that had taken root there. Lower Manhattan was experiencing an office building boom. SoHo seemed to be waiting in limbo for what might happen there next. And, as is usually true of zones of transition, property was neither maintained nor upgraded, but held in anticipation of future development.

All this despite some evidence that a significant percentage of SoHo's industry was still important to New York's economy. Rapkin's 1963 study argued that the South Houston Industrial Area, twelve blocks that are now part of SoHo, still contained a quite viable economic base, and provided needed employment opportunities for blue-collar workers. Good transportation was available, Rapkin noted: the district's western boundary opens on the entrance to the Holland Tunnel; on the east is the Manhattan Bridge to Brooklyn; subway and bus line stops are plentiful. But what was most salient in Rapkin's report was his assessment of the business activity in SoHo: "dingy exteriors . . . conceal the fact that the establishments operating within them are, for the most part, flourishing enterprises of considerable economic value to the city of New York" (Rapkin, 1963:9). According to Rapkin and others, the South Houston Industrial Area filled a critical niche in the economy of the city by supplying low-cost goods, as well as by recycling waste products from other industries. This assessment of the importance of SoHo's economic vitality was to be repeated again and again in the impending debates on the future of Lower Manhattan.

Although the data for Rapkin's study were gathered in 1963, we can see from table 2.1 that as late as 1973, the same blocks in SoHo still contained a large number of firms employing a substantial number of workers. Thus, Rapkin's 1963 recommendation that the area be supported as a commercial and industrial zone found continued support among some of the city planners and economists interviewed in this study from 1977 to 1981.

Rapkin proposed that remedial steps be taken to halt some of the more obvious signs of deterioration that he had documented. Some buildings needed extensive and expensive rehabilitation; others were in such bad shape that they needed to be razed and replaced.

Table 2.1   Business Establishments and Employees in a Twelve-Block Area in SoHo, 1962 and 1973[1]

	Business Establishments	Employees
1962[2]	651	12,671
1973[3]	459	8,394

[1] Neither Rapkin nor the City of New York included Broadway, the most industrialized and commercialized street in SoHo.
[2] Rapkin (1963:11–12).
[3] Estimate by the City Planning Commission, Department of City Planning, City of New York.

The city had been neglecting enforcing building codes; hence violations were rampant and conditions dangerous (Rapkin, 1963: 278–98). Some of the businesses were being managed by aging managerial staff whose heirs were seeking their fortunes elsewhere. As some of the older managers retired and some of the more marginal businesses began to close, the owners of the buildings found it increasingly difficult to replace their former commercial and industrial tenants. This was particularly true of the narrower buildings that could not accommodate new manufacturing technologies, which increasingly favored large horizontal spaces organized so that overhead cranes could shift machinery about with ease. These horizontal spaces are much more easily reorganized for production than are vertical spaces, which require movement between floors. The size and layout of production lines can be changed much more readily in a single horizontal space than in a multistoried factory (Rapkin, 1963:64–88). Thus many of the narrower lofts in SoHo were already obsolete as modern manufacturing space, and were being abandoned by commercial and industrial users. These narrow lofts, however, with their 1,500 and 2,000 square feet of space per floor, were already attracting a different population.

The changes taking place in Lower Manhattan were raising serious questions about the continuation of manufacturing there. Pressures from sources outside these manufacturing districts, as

■ The entrance to 102 Wooster in 1972 illustrates the kind of businesses that came to dominate SoHo. (Photo courtesy of Jane Collins Snowday.)

■ View from the rear of a SoHo loft. Note the shutters on windows and the general condition of the buildings. (Photo courtesy of Melvin Reichler and Judith Reichler.)

well as the conditions within, made some form of ecological succession more probable than it had been a few years before. The exact form of this succession was as yet unplanned and unpredicted. In the early 1950s, neither the city government nor private developers had initiated any large planning projects that specifically included these manufacturing areas. But although comprehensive planning had not as yet been pursued, an unplanned yet significant new use for SoHo's loft buildings had already been found.

The Invasion of the Pioneer Artists

"Pioneers," in both biological and human ecology, is a term applied to the early entrants into a new habitat. Their entrance is generally facilitated by certain characteristics that make it possible for them to adapt successfully to conditions found in this new environment. The concept is most often employed in ecology when the focus is on the initial stages of an invasion. What is frequently highlighted is the pioneers' impact upon the area invaded, which generates "site-modification," or change in the very environment that they are settling (Van Liere, 1977; Catton, 1980: 122; Freudenburg, 1985). The changes they produce in the area make it possible for other populations to follow; in the process, the initial pioneers are often ultimately displaced, as the developing community creates a new equilibrium. This, to some extent, is what happened in SoHo.

No one can accurately date the first time an artist moved into an industrial loft space to use it as a combination of work area and residence. George Macuinas, one of the founders of the art movement known as Fluxus and an early SoHo loft dweller, maintained that artists were living and working in the midtown garment district during World War II.[4] The well-known artist Robert Rauschenberg had a loft on Fulton Street in 1952. Of the various loft areas in Lower Manhattan that attracted artists in the early 1960s, SoHo became the major center for artists converting manufacturing lofts to work/residence spaces.

The residential population that first entered the lofts of SoHo was, then, composed almost exclusively of artists—painters, sculptors, dancers, and print, video, and film makers. The appeal of SoHo was the availability of large spaces at very low rents—spaces that could be used both for living and working. This appeal was enhanced by the artistic movements of the 1960s that required large spaces. The products of the Minimalists, Fluxus, Op, and Pop Art movements were often on a grand scale. The open spaces of the SoHo lofts permitted experiments with works that were thirty or more feet long and ten feet high. Such spaces provided opportunities to employ mixed media presentation. The floors of the SoHo lofts had such great bearing capacities that large sculptures could be undertaken on the upper floors, which could easily be reached by the large freight elevators in the buildings.

Although the creation of a single work of art may be an individual effort, artists have often clustered together to share ideas, offer mutual support, and provide a sympathetic audience for one another. The dynamics of rapid change in artistic styles over the past forty years have required that artists who want to remain current with the latest developments in art be close to the important galleries as well as accessible to others working in their particular field. Such artists feel that they have to "be within twenty minutes of the galleries." But New York's famed potential to provide anonymity was also valued: "It is the proximity or availability of fellow artists, not constant association with them, that makes New York different. The company is potentially congenial; the right people are not far off; but they can always be held at arm's length" (Rosenberg and Fliegel, 1965: 17–18).

SoHo had an appeal for artists (or "pull," as demographers describe the attractiveness of an area for in-migration): good working spaces that could be combined with living accommodations were available at low rents; there was a growing concentration of artists in Lower Manhattan, which provided a social and professional network for those pursuing artistic careers; and SoHo was located in Manhattan, where so much of the current history of contemporary art was being made (Guilbaut, 1983). These favorable elements drew artists to SoHo in increasing numbers, turning the initial invasion into a succession—with some special features.

The first of these features was that, while most cases of ecological succession have involved the replacement of one residential population by another (Aldrich, 1975; Duncan and Duncan, 1957; Cressey, 1938; Molotch, 1972), there was no residential population to be replaced in SoHo. Indeed, there was nothing that resembled a neighborhood or community there—no grocery stores, dry cleaning firms, barbershops, or any of the other services normally used by a residential population. If SoHo residents had children, there were no schools they could legally attend, because the zoned manufacturing area was not within any school district's boundaries. Those moving in were clearly, in the terms of Stratton's (1977) book title, "pioneering in the urban wilderness."

Pioneering in the Urban Wilderness

A second special feature in the succession process in SoHo at this period was the continued use of buildings that were there—buildings constructed for manufacturing and commercial, not for residential, use. The frequent pattern of tearing down outmoded structures—usually those built for special functions (as was the case in SoHo during the latter part of the nineteenth century)—did not reoccur. As a matter of fact, the architectural integrity and uniqueness of SoHo's buildings became one of the major arguments for rallying around the preservation of SoHo in the debates over proposed zoning and land use changes that occurred in the later phase of the process of succession (see Landmark Preservation Commission, 1973).

Another distinguishing feature of this succession in SoHo was that the population which initially moved in did so illegally and clandestinely. At the beginning of the period of succession, the area was zoned exclusively for industrial and commercial use. Although residential occupancy was illegal, it was abetted by a considerable degree of official tolerance for the incoming artist population (Millstein, 1962; Koch, 1976; Simpson, 1981). The unevenness of code enforcement, enabled by petty graft and the frequent collusion between owners and tenants, permitted a pattern of change which, at first, left the illegality of the movement relatively unchallenged.

While SoHo did not follow the usual process of residential invasion and succession, it did have some common elements associated with that process: e.g., those businesses that serve the original population either modify their services and merchandise, go out of business, or are replaced by new firms that can serve the incoming population (Aldrich and Reiss, 1976). In SoHo, a local liquor store broadened its line of wines to meet the tastes of the new residents (the owner reported that he saw himself as a link between the incoming artists and the residents in the nearby streets that bordered SoHo). A local paint shop began to carry special brushes, paints, and other materials in order to meet the requests of artists. Today, an inscription on the sidewalk in front of his store reads "Thanks, Alan Oldenburg"—the owner extended credit to this sculptor early in his career.

Other changes began to take place as artists came to dominate SoHo. Tourists began to frequent the area as it became known as a haven for artists, acquired a reputation for glamour, and became a site for urban adventure. A number of galleries opened to display the works of local artists. In 1968, Paula Cooper moved from her midtown location to open the first commercial gallery in SoHo (Gardner, 1974). Her gallery was quickly followed by a series of others: some with ties to uptown galleries, some that were founded by dealers solely involved with SoHo artists, and some established by artists working in SoHo themselves.

Art galleries were not the only new businesses being opened in SoHo. Shops specializing in prints and posters, art books, and artistic materials joined the bars, restaurants, and clothing stores that had begun to make street level SoHo an active retail commercial area. These galleries and stores provided employment for artists. As Simpson points out, only a few artists are able to make a living from their art, and most must seek supplementary employment (1981:53–72). Jobs in galleries, artists' supply stores, and teaching were used as a means of support by SoHo artists. Other new businesses provided employment specifically for artists: e.g.,

■ The photographer, Jane Collins Snowday, found this example of graffiti at 118–116 Wooster in 1972 as one reflection of SoHo's artistic vigor. (Photo courtesy of Jane Collins Snowday.)

one SoHo restaurant made an effort to recruit dancers, another actors ("serving a meal is a performance," the manager stated). These changes marked the transition of SoHo from an industrial area to a residential and artistic community with a new commercial base.

The Patterns of Loft Conversions in SoHo, 1965–77

There were 403 buildings classified as lofts by the Real Property Assessment Department of the City of New York in 1977. Data on each building include the 1973 assessed value, the size and dimensions of the building and the lot on which it stood, and the number of floors. Residential and commercial telephone listings were used to identify commercial and residential occupants in the buildings, the presence of a residential telephone being considered evidence of a conversion to residential use. The telephone listings were gathered at two-year intervals from 1965 to 1977. It should be assumed that some of the pioneer artists did not have telephones, and that some had unlisted ones to protect themselves from being detected by city housing officials (others made up fictitious commercial names to obtain commercial listings). The absence of data on those conversions was assumed to be random among the buildings and therefore does not distort the patterns revealed in the tables.

Table 2.2 indicates that about two-thirds of all loft buildings in SoHo have five or six floors, and that about 90 percent have seven or fewer. The preponderance of five- and six-story buildings is what gives SoHo its silhouette when viewed from the New Jersey side of the Hudson River—a valley between the tall buildings of the financial district of Lower Manhattan and the higher buildings north of Houston Street. The large number of low-rise buildings in this area also indicates the relative architectural stability it has enjoyed during the past 100 years, documenting that the high-rise construction that marks both midtown and Lower Manhattan did not impinge on this area. SoHo's profile reflects the land use patterns of housing and manufacturing in the late nineteenth century.

One way of gauging the extent of residential invasion in SoHo

Table 2.2   Distribution of the Number of Floors in SoHo Loft Buildings

Floors	Buildings	Percent
1	3	0.7
2	5	1.2
3	23	5.7
4	34	8.4
5	169	41.9
6	99	24.6
7	29	7.2
8	13	3.2
9	5	1.2
10	2	0.5
11	6	1.5
12	12	3.0
13	1	0.2
14	1	0.2
15	1	0.2

is simply to measure the number of residential telephones maintained in the loft buildings during the period from 1965 to 1977 (tables 2.3 and 2.4). As can be seen, the number of residential telephones in the area increased ninefold during the period, while the ratio of residential telephones to buildings more than doubled. If we look at the same data over each two-year interval, we can see an increase in residential telephones and a higher ratio of telephones to buildings. These data indicate not only a growing population of residents but also a growing concentration of residential tenants in individual buildings—a measure of increasing residential density within these buildings. The patterns appear to show that once a building was opened to conversion, there was a process of residential succession within that building itself. This process may have been encouraged because (1) the social network among artists recruited new occupants for buildings where conversions had begun; (2) building owners who were losing commercial tenants actively recruited residential tenants, even though it was illegal; and/or (3), those who were converting loft spaces illegally preferred to do so in those buildings that already had residential occupants, since they could assume the complicity of the landlord. Once the process had begun, the landlords, realizing that the

Table 2.3   Distribution and Ratio of Residential Telephones in SoHo Loft Buildings, 1965–77

Year	Residential Telephones	Buildings with Residential Telephones	Ratio of Residential Telephones to Buildings
1965	100	54	1.85:1
1967	127	63	2.03:1
1969	267	104	2.58:1
1971	357	131	2.72:1
1973	511	166	3.08:1
1975	712	204	3.49:1
1977	914	224	4.08:1

Table 2.4   Distribution of Residential Telephones in SoHo Loft Buildings, 1965–77

Telephones per Building	1965 (N=54)	1967 (N=63)	1969 (N=104)	1971 (N=131)	1973 (N=166)	1975 (N=204)	1977 (N=224)
1	53.7%	44.4%	33.7%	32.1%	30.1%	23.0%	14.3%
2	29.6	27.0	24.0	23.7	18.7	17.6	17.9
3	9.3	14.3	21.2	21.4	19.9	19.1	18.3
4	3.7	11.1	10.6	9.9	10.2	13.2	14.7
5	1.9	3.2	4.8	6.1	6.6	9.8	12.5
6	0	0	1.0	0	7.8	7.4	5.4
7	0	0	1.9	3.8	1.2	2.0	6.3
8	0	0	0	0	3.0	4.9	4.0
9	0	0	2.9	1.5	0.6	1.0	2.7
10	0	0	0	0.8	0.6	0.5	0.9
11	1.9	0	0	0	0	0	0
12	0	0	0	0	0.6	0	1.3
13	0	0	0	0	0	0.5	0.4
14	0	0	0	0.8	0.6	0.5	1.3
15	0	0	0	0	0	0.5	0

N = buildings

artists were good tenants, were less agressive in seeking new commercial tenants who were increasingly hard to come by anyway—after all, illegal tenants probably make fewer demands than legal tenants. All these forces operated synergistically to produce the results the data indicate.

By the end of the period studied, there were 914 residential telephones in 224 SoHo loft buildings; i.e., approximately 56 percent
of the loft buildings in SoHo had residential tenants. That there
were still 44 percent of SoHo loft buildings without residential
tenants indicates that the process of invasion had not eliminated
all commercial and industrial activity. Even though by this time
there had been changes in the zoning laws that permitted legal
conversion of loft spaces, a large number remained unconverted. It
can be assumed that many of the more successful businesses in
SoHo had long-term leases that protected them from displacement, that they were operating profitably, and that the largest ones
owned their buildings.

As can be seen from table 2.4, about 54 percent of the buildings
with residential telephones had only one in 1965. That proportion
steadily decreased over time until 1977, when only 14 percent of
the converted buildings had just one residential telephone. The
early low number of residential telephones supports the observation that conversions were a matter of individual initiative and not
the result of developers converting an entire building to residential
use (for a contrary opinion, see Zukin, 1982:135–40). Even by
1977, less than 50 percent of the buildings had more than three
telephones. The remaining spaces in these buildings were often
still occupied by commercial businesses. In 1977, there were still
1,181 commercial telephone listings and a lot of mixed use. The
problem posed by this continued mixed use became one of the
issues in the zoning debate, particularly in terms of "sandwiched"
residents, i.e., those occupying a residential floor between two
industrial floors.

There is general consensus among those who have studied loft
conversions that as manufacturing declined in New York the
smaller loft spaces were those least attractive to new commercial
tenants. These spaces, then, were first to become available to residential invasion. Table 2.5 contains data on the size of loft floors.
The measure used here is the number of square feet of a loft floor;
size has been grouped for ease of analysis. In 1965, about 61 percent
of all loft floors in SoHo were 3,000 square feet or less, and 87
percent of all conversions had been undertaken in buildings with

floors of this size. This pattern continued throughout the period, although by 1977 the proportion of buildings with this floor size had declined to 70 percent. The larger the space to be converted, the greater the cost of conversion and maintenance. However, there is a gradual increase in the size of lofts converted after 1971 (from 2,125 to 2,300 square feet) which coincides with changes in zoning laws. This increase also took place during the time when SoHo lofts had started to attract a more affluent, non-artist population.

Table 2.6 presents the data on the assessed value of a loft floor in converted buildings and, since actual rental figures are not available, represents the best approximation of rents. (It should be emphasized that rents are less precise than assessed value for measuring the market value of the buildings being converted, because of varying leases in the same buildings.)

The first lofts converted had the lowest assessed value. In 1965, 39 percent of the loft buildings that had been converted had an assessed floor value of $7,000 or less, while only 10 percent of the total buildings had floors assessed below that figure. As the process of loft conversions continued during the twelve-year period under consideration, conversion activity moved into the higher brackets of the 1973 assessments. This can be most easily seen in the shift in the median assessed value of a building, as well as a floor. In 1965, the median assessed value of a SoHo loft building that had some conversion activity was $45,000. This increased to just over $60,000 at the end of the period studied. The assessed value of a floor also increased from $9,012 to $11,676.

These data imply that as the process of conversion gathered momentum, those making conversions probably were also more affluent, supporting the general contention that higher-income groups began moving into SoHo as it developed, a pattern that is consistent with those found in urban residential neighborhoods that have been gentrified (Clay, 1979; Gale, 1977; Laska and Spain, 1980).

The ecological process of invasion-succession begins as a response to an alteration in an environment which opens up niches for

Table 2.5 Distribution of SoHo Loft Buildings with Residential Telephones by Floor Size, 1965–77

Floor Size in Square Feet	1965 (N=54)	1967 (N=63)	1969 (N=104)	1971 (N=131)	1973 (N=166)	1975 (N=204)	1977 (N=224)	All Buildings (N=403)
Under 1000	25.9%	23.8%	20.2%	16.0%	16.3%	14.2%	14.7%	13.2%
1000–1999	46.3	49.2	51.0	51.9	46.4	42.6	42.4	35.0
2000–2999	14.8	12.7	12.5	15.3	15.1	13.2	12.9	12.4
3000–3999	3.7	3.2	6.7	7.6	7.8	10.3	9.8	9.9
4000–5999	1.9	3.2	4.8	3.8	6.0	10.3	9.8	9.2
6000–6999	1.9	1.6	0	0.8	2.4	2.9	3.1	5.7
7000–7999	3.7	3.2	2.9	3.1	3.0	3.9	3.6	4.2
8000–8999	0	0	0	0	0	0	0	0.7
9000–9999	0	0	1.0	0.8	1.2	1.5	1.8	2.2
10,000–10,999	1.9	3.2	1.0	0.8	1.2	0.5	1.3	3.2
11,000–14,999	0	0	0	0	0.6	0.5	0.4	2.0
15,000–19,999	0	0	0	0	0	0	0	1.0
20,000 and over	0	0	0	0	0	0	0	0.5
Median Size	2125	2126	2125	2126	2250	2299	2300	

N = buildings

Table 2.6   Distribution of SoHo Loft Buildings with Residential Telephones by 1973 Assessed Value of a Floor, 1965–77

Assessed Value in Dollars	1965 (N=54)	1967 (N=63)	1969 (N=104)	1971 (N=131)	1973 (N=166)	1975 (N=204)	1977 (N=224)	All Buildings (N=403)
Under 4000	5.6%	4.8%	3.8%	3.1%	2.4%	2.5%	2.2%	2.5%
4000–4999	16.7	15.9	12.5	9.9	7.8	6.4	5.8	3.7
5000–6999	5.6	4.8	3.8	4.6	3.6	3.4	3.6	3.7
7000–7999	11.1	14.3	15.4	15.3	13.9	11.8	11.6	7.9
8000–8999	3.7	4.8	6.7	9.9	9.0	8.8	9.4	8.4
9000–9999	7.4	9.5	11.5	9.9	9.6	9.3	9.4	7.0
10,000–10,999	7.4	7.9	7.7	6.9	7.2	6.4	5.8	4.7
11,000–15,999	22.2	17.5	16.3	20.6	21.1	21.6	21.9	20.6
16,000–20,999	7.4	6.3	9.6	7.6	7.8	9.8	10.3	10.2
21,000–25,999	3.7	4.8	3.8	3.8	7.2	8.3	8.5	8.9
26,000–30,999	3.7	4.8	5.8	6.1	5.4	5.9	4.9	6.5
31,000–35,999	0	0	0	0	1.2	1.0	0.9	0.2
36,000–40,999	3.7	3.2	1.0	0.8	0.6	2.5	2.7	3.2
41,000–45,999	1.9	1.6	1.0	0.8	2.4	2.0	0.9	4.2
46,000–50,999	0	0	1.0	0.8	0.6	0.5	1.3	1.5
Over 51,000	0	0	0	0	0	0	0.9	5.0
Median								
Median Assessed Value: Building	45,000	45,125	45,250	47,850	54,850	59,850	60,050	
Median Assessed Value: Floor	9,012	8,994	8,994	9,378	10,002	11,491	11,676	

N = buildings

a new or different population. The pioneer artists who invaded manufacturing loft spaces in SoHo and other areas of Lower Manhattan were such a population. As their numbers, and the number of loft buildings they occupied, increased, the process of succession in these areas began to be apparent. At the same time, both without and within SoHo and the rest of Lower Manhattan, there were complex social dynamics operating that had potential consequences for the future development of the area.

3 ■ The Social Environment of SoHo's Development

Overview

Ecological succession and other social dynamics operating during SoHo's development did not arise solely from spontaneous social combustion ignited by the area's internal energy. These dynamics were strongly affected by social forces already operating beyond SoHo's borders. The effects of these forces filtered through SoHo's structure and generated new social configurations, reaffirming a basic principle of cultural diffusion: a receiving society will adapt a new idea, process, or tool to fit into its own social patterns, even though the adaptation may produce a fundamental change in those patterns.

In a complex social matrix like that found in SoHo, with exogenous and endogenous forces at work concomitantly, it is impossible to tease out which of these forces produced which results. There are no discrete sequences of stimulus and response, but a continuous pattern of interaction that prohibits any attempt to establish causal linkages between specific forces producing change and the specific changes themselves. In retrospect, the progression of events appears linear and predictable, but that is an illusion of hindsight. SoHo's patterns of social organization could have developed into several different configurations as the process unfolded, depending upon plan, choice, and chance; any of these resultant patterns could have been given a reasonable theoretical interpretation.

The impact on SoHo of the changes in manufacturing technology and the new forms of economic organization in the United States has already been noted. Other technological changes were also occurring that made SoHo vulnerable to the form succession took in its loft spaces—the new uses of technology in art. At the same time, new life-styles were challenging traditional approaches to housing, family formation, and gender roles. Part of SoHo's growing attraction as a tourist center was the presence of these life-styles, dramatically exemplified by SoHo's residents. In addition, the mass media had adopted a new approach to social reporting that legitimated the struggles of those demanding social justice in the 1960s and 1970s. The SoHo artists were but one group among many that benefited from this new journalism, which helped redefine urban politics, particularly in those older cities that were losing their traditional industrial base, to include preservation and restoration as part of their future development. The abandoned, decayed, and deteriorated neighborhoods of many cities were being discovered and refurbished by a new generation of urban dwellers. New York City had encouraged these efforts in its support of "brownstone" renovations in several neighborhoods in Manhattan. The process of gentrification was not, however, initially a part of SoHo's development, but came to play a more important role as the artist pioneers settled this urban frontier (Hudson, 1984).

Art, Technology, and Politics

The contemporary link between art and technology was forged with the establishment of the Bauhaus in Germany in the 1920s. Essentially, the Bauhaus ideology rejected the concept that modern industrial society must produce alienation. The design of buildings and their contents could be aesthetically pleasing; the buildings could be placed in well-designed settings; and the result could contribute to individual self-worth. In its own organization, the Bauhaus sought to eliminate class distinctions between management and labor, as well as between the worker and the artist. Production was to be a shared experience in which the process of production had equal status with the product itself. Everyday items could be well designed and mass-produced. In 1913, Marcel Duchamp had called attention to the aesthetic appeal of such items as the bicycle wheel, steel comb, typewriter cover, and urinal. Such a focus was predicated on the belief that art was not just for an elite, that museums were not the sole repositories of art—the enjoyment and appreciation of art could be part of everyone's daily experience. This belief was reaffirmed by American artists in the 1960s and 1970s.

The Bauhaus fell victim to the Nazis in the early 1930s, and its distinguished faculty was dispersed to Western democracies—a large number finding refuge in the United States. The prestigious positions they found in American universities gave them podia from which to expound the Bauhaus ideology (Wolfe, 1983; Davis, 1973).

The rise of Nazi Germany and the preparations for World War II had other political consequences for art besides the dispersal of the Bauhaus faculty. In 1935, the Russian Communist Party launched a program known as the Popular Front, aimed at uniting opposition to fascism, which sought support among intellectuals, writers, and artists. Communist parties in Western nations had to mute their more strident attacks on capitalism to encourage bourgeois participation in the Popular Front. The important point for artists in all of this was that "for the first time in American history, it seemed that writers, theater people, and painters were not out of step with society, that their social role was finally being recognized. The Popular Front in which the artist played a part in a sense represented the end of his alienation, the first step toward participation in and acceptance by society in its common endeavor" (Guilbaut, 1983:19).

Incredible tensions developed within the left at the end of the 1930s, resulting in the formation of innumerable splinter groups and dissident factions: vituperative criticisms and personal feuds were common. Nonetheless, the political thrust of the left was not completely blunted. World War II brought a moratorium on some of the more vicious infighting among the leftist groups. Russia became a valiant ally in the war against fascism, and the basic antagonism between Russian communism and Western capitalism was repressed for political purposes. At end of World War II, however, animosities were renewed, as reflected in such postwar coinage as the Cold War and the Iron Curtain. The left-wing sympathies among some American artists made their work suspect to those who were to speak of the postwar period as "The American Century" (Guilbaut, 1983:60–61). The artistic values of the Popular Front and the wartime support for Russia were replaced with a more American-centered art that was more in keeping with the new values of the "vital center" that came to dominate American politics (Guilbaut, 1983:189–92).

Between 1946 and 1948, however, there was a short period of real diversity in the political debates in America. There was a rejection of the "left-wing uniformity of the New Deal of the thirties" and the conformity which would eventually dominate the 1950s. "Not only political but also artistic commitments were being questioned: there were battles, splits, shifts, reorganizations, and redefinitions, even as new positions began to solidify" (Guilbaut, 1983:105). The new political positions called for a new art form, and Abstract Expressionism evolved to meet the requirements: it was basically American in origin and development; its politics were essentially safe, i.e., without radical political content; and it could be used by the government to exemplify the growing cultural hegemony of the United States that paralleled the nation's recognized political hegemony in the world. Abstract Expressionism established the United States as the new center of art, replacing the older European centers, particularly Paris (Guilbaut, 1983; Sandler, 1970). It was referred to as the "international style," as if to indicate that American artistic leadership crossed the political frontiers of nation states, just as American political and economic power achieved worldwide dominance.[1]

Perhaps even more important, Abstract Expressionism was a very personal art form. In its execution, the creative process was an individual effort, and the energy that gave the process direction came from within the individual, not from the collective force of a Bauhaus. It made use of a limited number of techniques and avoided any attempt to use new technologies. Modern industrial technology's power had been revealed in its most destructive form during World War II, and artists, like many others, viewed it with some suspicion, rejecting the earlier Bauhaus mandate to combine art and technology. New York City, the home of Abstract Expressionism, became the leader in the world of art, a magnet drawing those who wanted to be at the epicenter of artistic activity.

As the 1950s neared their end, the tools, materials, and techniques artists were using were changing again. The separation between art and technology that had marked the immediate postwar period gave way to a closer collaboration between the two, with strong, new sentiments for the Bauhaus philosophy being evidenced. Artistic production once more involved collaboration between artists and technicians. Any form of production that begins to employ more complex technologies requires new spatial dimensions and greater interdependence among those engaged in the productive process. The celebrated individualism of Abstract Expressionism came to be replaced by emphasis on more cooperative efforts and a stronger sense of community.

Abstract Expressionists were usually content to work with the most traditional materials: oil, paint, and canvas. "Contrary forces were at work, however, in the very heart of the New York School. Barnett Newman started both to 'spray' paint on the canvas and to deal with clean, self-defined forms reminiscent of the Bauhaus and DeStijl" (Davis, 1973:34). But this was merely the tentative first step; a flood of new materials and technologies came to be employed in artistic production during the late 1950s and 1960s (for more on the relationship between art and technology, see Becker, 1982:311). The list includes, but is not limited to, the Olsen-Belar electronic sound synthesizer; micro and aerial photography; the high-vacuum optical coating machine; explosive forming; computers; television; vinyls; new resins; laser holograms; "clean rooms"; and acrylic paints.

Artists' employment of new technologies fostered development of craft relations. These technologies are complicated, their development and improvement often rapid. If the artist were to keep pace with technology, he or she would need to establish links to those industrial engineers and inventors who were creating these innovations. These links were not that difficult to forge; ever since the 1930s, a number of artists had been trained as engineers and technicians. Their involvement in artistic production helped develop a mutual respect and shared language among artists and engineers. It opened avenues of communication which presented engineers with interesting problems and brought innovations quickly into the artists' studios (Davis, 1973:71).

These channels of communication were not merely informal or fortuitous. "By 1966, a pivotal year in American art in any case, the idea that technology represented an alien, anti-human, anti-art force had been cast in doubt. In retrospect, the time appears to have been ripe for the project launched by Robert Rauschenberg and Swedish engineer Bill Kluver, that culminated in the founding of Experiments in Art and Technology, Inc." (Davis, 1973:67). The initial group included engineers from Bell Laboratories in New Jersey, where Kluver had worked. Such intentional inclusion of technicians in artistic production resulted not only in the production of various artistic works that depended upon complex technology, but also in the reinforcement of the idea that artistic production involved labor that could be organized in a shop. This idea was not new. The influential sculptor David Smith had called his 1930s studio the Terminal Iron Works, and in the 1960s Andy Warhol called his studio The Factory.

This emphasis on how and where art was made also led to a new emphasis on the materials being used. Rather than ignoring their character, the artist called attention to them in a way reminiscent of Marcel Duchamp. The materials were often what could be gleaned from the streets: the found objects in the environment. Kaprow, who is credited with inventing the "happening," "stood for the uninhibited use in art of the materials 'found' in the environment, an attitude derived largely from his study of Zen Buddhism" (Davis, 1973:35). Finding objects to use became important for artists; therefore, an environment that offered rich sources of found materials attracted them.

The point here is not the broad implications of these various trends for art and American culture, but rather that their collective influences commingled in SoHo to contribute to its development as an artistic center. These forces were not simply modified to fit SoHo's particular setting, but were transformed, reenforced, and strengthened by the resident artists. The trends and changes in SoHo, other artistic centers, and the larger society were synchronistic—influences and innovations flowed in several directions simultaneously.

The connection between the SoHo artists' ideology and the tradition of the Bauhaus, particularly the link between workers and artists, has already been noted. SoHo was not simply a place with cheap, large spaces that could be converted into artists' studios at minimal expense. SoHo was a blue-collar manufacturing area: an industrial section of the city where the streets were crowded daily with trucks and workers. This was a place where hard work was done and respected. Artistic production requires intensive labor, and there was a recognition by the blue-collar workers that artists did work hard, even if they worked odd hours. There were no distinctions made by those who worked in SoHo based upon social status or occupation—at least among those who "toiled."

Commercial shops in SoHo welcomed artists who needed assistance in their productions. Welding companies gave advice to sculptors on various techniques. Print shops helped artists solve problems of lithographic production. And at the southern border of SoHo was the western end of Canal Street. This end of Canal Street is home to many hardware stores, surplus outlets, and discount houses. "Through its pathways, one strolls in the cool of the evening. There are crates of power tools, barrels of pliers, rack upon rack of plexiglass, whole floors crammed with cheap office furniture. Here on Canal Street, lofts are furnished, works and careers are conceived, souls are soothed. From Canal Street, and its like, the improbably elegance of the place has been assembled" (Koch, 1976:121).

But it was not only the stores along Canal Street that furnished the artists with supplies. The marginal businesses in SoHo often

■ Melvin Reichler, a sociologist and early SoHo resident, took this picture on Greene Street looking north. It represented for him "the unromantic, but very real sense of SoHo as a place to live and work." (Photo courtesy of Melvin Reichler and Judith Reichler.)

■ Workers taking a break in a manufacturing loft in 1971. The height of the windows in these buildings can be judged from the workers sitting on the ledge. (Photo courtesy of The New-York Historical Society, New York City.)

■ The tall building is at 343 Canal Street. The street-level stores indicate some of the places where artists found the materials they used for their work. (Photo courtesy of The New-York Historical Society, New York City.)

discarded interesting materials that artists found useful for their work. Pieces of metal, wire, and corrugated cardboard found their way to the artists' lofts. Picking over the discards from these businesses became a regular nocturnal activity for those living in SoHo. There even developed a certain etiquette governing the process of pawing through the discards. The first rule was not to approach any trash containers while someone else was selecting objects. It was also de rigeur to put the trash back into the containers when one had finished making choices. When this custom was violated and certain businesses no longer put their trash out, some artists were invited into the shops to select the refuse materials they wanted. When asked why they chose such materials, artists like Dan Flavin, who worked with fluorescent bulbs responded: "I just used them because they were handy, cheap, neutral, and available" (Davis, 1973:44).

The employment of found materials in artistic production reflected the artists orientation to the community in which they worked. A quotation attributed to Rauschenberg might have been their slogan: "I felt as though I were collaborating with the neighborhood" (Davis, 1973:37).

The movement of these artists into SoHo's industrial spaces also coincided with important methodological changes in the production and sale of art. As New York emerged as the art center of the world after World War II, New York based critics, journals, galleries, and museums became the arbiters of artistic taste. Art classes in New York colleges and universities drew important figures in contemporary art, both as teachers and as students. Art production and sale in New York became an important export industry. "In concept, the arts can be considered in rather conventional economic terms. On the one hand, the arts comprise a producing 'industry' (a peculiar industry, to be sure), a source of jobs and income for participants in the production process, sellers of supplies and services to the arts-producing firms, and operators of ancillary activities, like restaurants in the theater district of Manhattan. On the other hand, the arts are a collection of consumer goods, enjoyed by households as audiences, spectators, and amateur participants" (Netzer, 1978:51:2). SoHo came to be the center of this industry, with associated tourist and customer services that altered its street life while providing work for some artists.

The concept of the artist-industrialist took visible form in the development of SoHo. SoHo's unique features have been internationally recognized. To celebrate the bicentennial of the United States in 1976, the Akademie der Künste and the Berliner Festwochen produced an art show exclusively of SoHo artists. "Here an essential stimulation towards renewed culture work, towards a changed comprehension of the artists themselves could develop, as artists in all fields lived closely together in SoHo and were forced to look at the social urban problems of their environment" (Eckhardt and Düttman, 1976:5).

The increase in the production of art was paralleled by a growth in its market. One of the by-products of using new technologies was that art could be disseminated to larger audiences than was previously possible. Low-cost reproductions no longer were equated with kitsch. Increased production lowered costs, and ownership of good art was not restricted to a limited elite (Davis, 1973:171–72). Some artists developed kits that others assembled, not in predetermined ways such as painting-by-numbers, but in creative ways that gave the assembler a sense of artistic production (Davis, 1973:52). There were closer ties between art and its audience. The "happenings"—those "spontaneous" productions that had no predetermined structure—were one clear attempt to increase the participation of the audience in the production of art.

"Modernism in art is no longer the adventurous or defiant probe of a vanguard of artists and intellectuals occupying an enclave in a city busy with its own affairs. The isolation of advanced art from society has been overcome, largely, it would seem, through the increased instability of society itself. Today, extremist forms in art are everywhere accepted as a reflex to the incomprehensible in science and technology to the bafflement of philosophy" (Rosenberg, 1964:210). The idea that art is not something distant and unknowable makes art more relevant to our daily lives. The incorporation of everyday objects into art has given us a sense that art is all about us. We are all familiar with some of the materials used in modern art: they appear on our kitchen shelves, in our living rooms, on the television screen, and at our workplaces. The increased presence of art objects in contemporary buildings, and the associated support for art by major corporations, makes access to art routine.

We may conclude, then, that the spirit of the Bauhaus had found a sanctuary in the United States. It had to weather the political storms of the 1930s, 1940s, and 1950s before its ideals were accepted—and they were not accepted emphatically by everyone (see Wolfe, 1981). Nor were they adopted without being modified by American tastes, values, and ideas.

While the Bauhaus spirit had a good deal of influence on American art, it did not wholly dominate the artistic movements of the postwar period. Abstract Expressionism was conceived and nurtured in the United States. It made the United States the leader in contemporary art, a position it has not relinquished since. Within the United States, New York has dominated the art world, and in New York SoHo has become the home for contemporary art movements and artists—both physically and ideologically. But SoHo is not only an area that has housed artists and given birth to new artistic trends; it is also an area in which a new approach to urban housing was developed, a new life-style was created, and a new model for the urban tourist was born.

Trends in Life-Style and Tourism

The political and social turmoil that marked the immediate postwar period in the United States subsided during the 1950s. There were some remaining turbulences that sent disturbing social ripples through the calm waters of American society—for example, the "howls" of the Beat writers and the raucous sound of rock 'n' roll—but for the most part, the period was marked by conservatism, prosperity, and social values that rewarded conformity, corporate loyalty, and traditional goals. All of this was reflected in migration to the suburbs, and norms in housing and interior decoration that reflected the dominance of the nuclear family, including gender segregation that affirmed male superiority in the home and workplace.

The period was clearly marked by the increasing white middle-class exodus from older cities. The changing distribution of population was also accompanied by changes in the location of commerce and industry. Older cities came under a cloud; they were regarded as outmoded social structures that housed the poor, the aged, the minorities, and others who could not make the successful transition to modern American life. While there were massive attempts to stem the tide of urban decay, these efforts did not restore cities to their former glory, or even alleviate their more serious problems. Cities were no longer accorded the respect they once had as the centers of innovation, creativity, and vitality.

Although urban life appeared moribund during the 1950s and early 1960s, there were countertrends that began to develop, giving cities renewed life. A particular manifestation of these nascent trends was the growth of loft living and the life-style associated with it. In addition, some urban areas provided recreation emphasizing urban flavor rather than imitating suburban taste. SoHo was such an area, and loft living, life-style, and tourism came to play a significant role in its growth and development.

Making homes of the factory lofts of SoHo produced a new interior design for living. Loft space was not divided into a series of rooms, specialized areas, and personal territories. There was a great deal of variation in how lofts were converted for residential use; the common denominator, however, was the emphasis on large open areas. Lofts, with the same number of square feet as many American homes, are frequently entirely free of interior walls; a usual exception is the bathroom, but even that is open in some lofts. All lofts have high ceilings ranging up to fifteen feet. Areas for eating, sleeping, entertaining, and other routine functions are widely scattered. The following cases are extreme, in that they represent some of the most dramatic examples of loft living and life-style; however, since they are taken from the mass media, they indicate how the style of loft living was being presented to the public.

A flatbed elevator opens onto polished hardwood and hanging greenery. The whole vista is partitioned by track-lighting into living, working and dining space. There are modular couches and Breuer chairs; a work in monumental burlap covers an entire wall. The owner greets you with cashews and Perrier. She's a buyer in the garment center. Her boss doesn't understand why she won't live on Third Avenue. But what good is the East Side if you can't get into Regine's? And besides her shrink lives down the block. (Goldstein, 1977:24)

$1,200 king-size bathtubs and enough hot water to fill them, acres of exotic plants, uniformed housekeepers, children in private schools, Chinese chefs, Touch-tone phones, closed-circuit TV surveillance, light dimmers, ice makers, trash compactors, industrial vacuum cleaners, Steinway pianos, antique pool tables, imported eighteenth-century beams, 24-foot-long leather sofas, original Rietveld chairs, Directoire settees, foundations, fireplaces, and more Bloomingdale's. And the most middle-class hang-up of all—good housekeeping, and I don't mean the magazine. (Kron, 1974:54)

Most people have to go outdoors to jog. Neils Diffrient and his wife, Helena Hernmarck, do their jogging in their loft, running past her looms and his drawing board, around the Ping Pong table, the open kitchen area, the free standing fireplace and the open bedroom, while Thomas, the ginger cat, gets out of the way by bedding down on a table full of yarn. . . . However, for all its high ceilings, while walls, and vast space, the Diffrients' loft hasn't the barren look of a gymnasium. The tools of their separate crafts form some of the furniture and certainly most of the decorative aspects of the loft. (Taylor, 1977:C–8)

These examples illustrate loft living and life-style at its most complete and polished. Their variety demonstrates the creative uses the tenants made of such spaces. Large numbers of loft dwellers, however, made only modest changes to handle the necessities of living: e.g., repairing broken windows, installing toilets that worked, and covering up holes in the floor. A few created museums of modernity.

The methods of dividing living and work space varied, as the quotations above indicate. Living and work spaces often overlapped. In other lofts there were clear separations. One loft owner installed three overhead garage doors to separate his work space

■ A corner of Jane Collins Snowday's loft after it had been cleaned and before it had been converted to residential use. (Photo courtesy of Jane Collins Snowday.)

■ Snowday's loft after it had been professionally decorated. The story that accompanied this photo included the following: "*A Lofty Approach to Living* . . . in New York City's SoHo artist district. This is the downtown retreat of a single lady with a high pressure job at one of the Big Apple's most important ad agencies." (Quoted with permission. Photo courtesy of Jane Collins Snowday.)

from his family's living space. These could be opened at the end of the work day so that the spaciousness of the entire loft could be enjoyed by all. A printmaker kept his nineteenth-century press at the back of the loft: because of his very neat work habits, there was no jarring contrast between the living and work areas. In part, it was this variety of styles that led to the public attention and popularity enjoyed by loft living. In 1977, the *Village Voice* made the following assessment: "The presence of unified avant garde within a single neighborhood has profoundly altered the New York style, from the way we furnish our homes (high tech) to the way we envision public space. Even the decision to wear a solid T-shirt over painter's pants, reflects the SoHo aesthetic—combining the minimal with the found" (Goldstein, 1977:22).

Loft living as a style became a recurrent subject for the media. A sampling of titles from contemporary magazine articles gives some of the flavor of this coverage: "Living Big in a Loft" (*Life*); "SoHo: Brave New Bohemia" (*Art News*); "SoHo: The Most Exciting Place to Live in the City" (*New York Magazine*); "Still Funky but oh so chic SoHo" (*Art News*); "Loft Living: Can You Make it on the Urban Frontier?" (*Apartment Life*). SoHo was even chosen as the locale for the film *An Unmarried Woman*.

A great deal of this publicity was accompanied by photographs showing loft conversions of different sorts. Although many of the articles were somewhat cautionary—pointing out the pitfalls in converting loft spaces, the perils of living illegally, and so on—the usual conclusion was that loft living was new, exciting, and "where it was happening." What had started out as a movement into an industrial and commercial district by a few poor artists generated an alternative life-style that would be imitated in inner cities throughout the United States.[2]

But the kind of publicity associated with it in New York gave the process national prominence. This sense of being at the center was very much a part of SoHo's self-image: the feeling that SoHo had shown the way, that SoHo was more authentic than its imitators, that it had become an ultimate urban experience—all contributed to an attitude of neighborhood pride, and a bit of smugness, among its residents.

An area devoted to the production and distribution of art must attract potential buyers from beyond its boundaries. Artists, particularly those who produce works that need to be seen, require audiences that can visit their displays. "Art sales accelerated through the 1960s and peaked in 1968, 1973, and 1979. The expansive atmosphere prompted many uptown gallery staffers to enter the market as entrepreneurs themselves, relying initially upon artists and buyers they could take from their old employers and setting up their new businesses in SoHo where commercial rents were far less than those in the uptown galleries" (Simpson, 1981:15). This combination of an increasing market for art and the shift in the market from uptown to downtown provided the first impetus for the growth of a tourist industry. If one adds to this the appeal of an offbeat, bizarre new life-style, tourism was a natural development.

So the outcome of these combined developments was at least understandable, if not inevitable: SoHo became one of the major New York tourist attractions. By 1978, a 274-page SoHo guidebook had been published, complete with street maps, suggested walking tours, and a directory of eighty-five art galleries, twenty-five restaurants, and sixty-five shops and boutiques. In the huckster style of such books, Seigfried and Seeman provided the eager tourist with this opening description: "You are now about to enter SoHo, one of the most exciting 'new' neighborhoods in New York city" (1978:3). SoHo was in. In 1981, a novel entitled *SoHo* (Byrd) appeared, further enhancing the romantic image of the area. In 1984, the *New York Review of Books* published *The SoHoiad: or the Masque of Art: A Satire in Heroic Couplets,* by the pseudonymous Junius Secundus, which satirized many of SoHo's pretensions and mythological history. This work did not diminish SoHo's luster, but rather added to its notoriety.

Simpson comments on the dilemmas involved in trying to develop as an artist while supporting oneself. "The career choice of fine arts is difficult to defend on economic grounds. Artists typically earn low incomes and experience the stress of having to earn most of this income from either low-paying, casual work or from quasi careers which continually threaten to take over their fine art

■ The storefront of a chic shop in SoHo. Notice the nineteenth-century cast-iron pillars. (Photo courtesy of Melvin Reichler and Judith Reichler.)

identity. Artists find themselves backing into other jobs to supply the necessary income and acquiring secondary identities as art teachers, cab drivers, or script coordinators in the production of television" (1981:58).

Tourism also provides opportunities for employment. SoHo artists, many of whom were seeking some means of supporting themselves until they could make a living from their art, took advantage of these opportunities. For example, one restaurant owner described her service of food as a "performance," and employed only actors as waiters. In another restaurant, the waiters were all dancers. There were a number of employment opportunities that fitted the odd working hours and habits of artists, and these mutually beneficial relationships gave SoHo part of its unique character (Hudson, 1978).

The growth of tourism in SoHo was not welcomed equally by all residents and observers. Ratcliff's essay, "SoHo: Disneyland of the Aesthete?" (1978), is representative of the criticism aimed at the success of SoHo as a tourist attraction. "SoHo," he wrote, "offers too much in the way of 'fun boutiques,' 'interesting restaurants,' and 'unusual nightspots' to raise any question about value in art— and it's not the purpose of a tourist attraction to raise questions, anyway. A tourist attraction is supposed to provide entertainment. For a culturally-aspiring segment of the general public, that is what SoHo does" (1978:70). Ratcliff may have been right, and many resident artists might now agree with him. But the changes described here seem to have been almost inevitable, not simply because art and tourism make a profitable combination, but also because the visibility so directly sought and celebrated by artists—even their successful fight to legalize their residence—inevitably invited tourism.

There are, of course, styles in tourism. SoHo is not a ruin to be admired from a bus, but a place where people mix and mingle for purposes other than cultural enrichment. Its galleries, bars, restaurants, and shops provide safe places for urban sociability. While slightly offbeat, the area is not outrageous, and decidedly not violent. Art galleries and art museums give the area a sense of place that promotes civility and public decorum.

SoHo is an example of the general pattern of new life-styles and tourism that have developed in many of our older inner cities in the last ten years. These cities now have recreational areas that have a strong appeal for those seeking an urban experience. What distinguishes SoHo from a number of other variations of these patterns is its unplanned and unintended evolution into such an area. In other neighborhoods in New York, as well as in other cities, such recreational areas were the products of developers who capitalized on what SoHo had demonstrated—that cities could still provide locations for excitement and entertainment.

The Role of the Mass Media

As has been shown, the media was very sympathetic to the changes taking place in SoHo—not only to the revitalization of the area and the new life-style of loft living, but also to the artistic ferment being generated. Despite initial heavy opposition from the city itself, SoHo's transformation was facilitated by the mass media, which perceived its role as championing the struggle of artists to secure themselves a place in American society.

The pervasive impact the mass media has on our society hardly needs documentation. We are so accustomed to the media's continuous presence in our lives that when we are cut off from its communications, we experience a sense of deprivation. Each of us may select different elements from its many offerings, but none of us is immune to its overall impact. Changes in the media's style also influence our perceptions, expectations, and attitudes. The shift from yellow journalism to more "objective" reporting after World War I led us to expect—even come to demand—value-neutral news reporting.

Janowitz (1977) has pointed to a more recent change in media focus: from objective "gatekeeping" to "advocacy" journalism. The gatekeeping model was regarded as the proper professional approach to the news from the 1920s until the early 1960s. "It represented the belief that the scientific method was productive in various sections of society, and that it had broad substantive and cultural relevance for the journalist" (Janowitz, 1977:74). Gatekeeping journalists sought to emphasize objectivity in their reporting. The professionalism embodied in this position was attacked in the mid-1960s by those who wanted journalism to become more socially conscious. Objectivity in and of itself was questioned as the only measure of professional reporting: "objective" facts were still selectively reported; the media could only subscribe to impartiality, not guarantee it. Rather than maintaining objectivity, "the task of the journalist was to represent the viewpoints and interests of competing groups" (Janowitz, 1977:74). This change in media focus had important consequences for SoHo when it became a battleground on which artists and city officials fought over the issue of loft conversions. Social justice, urban preservation, and individual worth were matched against government indifference, urban decay, and bureaucratic rigidity in the media's coverage of the struggle.

Advocacy journalism was being widely practiced by New York City's media when loft conversions became news. The art movements themselves, with their ideological programmatic aims, e.g., to make art available and affordable to a larger public as audience, were obviously subjects of social import. Artists who were converting lofts illegally, yet "saving" an urban area, provided advocate journalists with a moral cause. An embattled artist struggling heroically against government bureaucracies and corporate wealth had great journalistic possibilities. After all, the city and private developers had not been very successful in stabilizing or reviving inner city neighborhoods, while the loft converters of SoHo seemed to be doing it. The neighborhood itself had vigor and vitality that contrasted with the sterility of areas around public housing projects: projects that were the unsuccessful efforts of cities to answer the need for new housing. The efforts of loft-converting artists were fresh alternatives to stale proposals. They were creative, inventive, and romantic.

New York had already lost one art community—Greenwich Village. It had passed through so many transformations that it was no longer a center for art production or residence. Indiscriminate commercialization, the extraordinary rise in housing costs, and the incursions of institutions like New York University had destroyed much of its original appeal. Certainly there were still streets with elegant townhouses, carefully restored and preserved. But these residences did not house aspiring artists. If New York was to remain a cultural center, it needed room for innovative artists, particularly artists who had not yet achieved economic security. SoHo appeared to be a natural location for such innovators.

As might be expected, the strongest support for SoHo as an artist colony came from the liberal press, the *New York Times*, the *New York Post*, and the *Village Voice* in particular. From 1961 through 1983 approximately 175 articles reviewed in these papers reported on various aspects of loft conversion in Lower Manhattan. There were stories and articles on such diverse topics as the political and practical problems of loft conversions; the new life-style in lofts; the art being produced; the lives of the artists; the new stores that were opening; as well as, of course, restaurant reviews. The central theme of these articles was always in the major key, positive about what was happening in the loft areas. In the early 1960s, the major concern was that these loft spaces represented "the last resort left to artists as studios," and that if these artists did not find space in which to work, New York would lose its prominence as a center of artistic production.

The growth of SoHo as a community was also featured, and making artist occupancy of lofts legal was a recurrent editorial theme. The constant worry expressed in the media was that artists might be priced out of SoHo if the regulations favoring artist occupancy were not maintained. The artists were presented as an embattled minority attempting to produce work under trying conditions: the problems involved in making lofts habitable, the difficulties in dealing with municipal bureaucrats, and the effects of gentrification on the price structure of loft spaces all received sympathetic media coverage.

None of these newspaper articles was opposed to the changes taking place in the loft districts. There was concern over the possible loss of blue-collar jobs, but this concern was frequently juxtaposed with evidence suggesting that the artists and industrial residents could share the same area. After all, the artists were not seeking to displace viable businesses. The only villains ever identified were the developers, who might displace both businesses and artists. The 1960s and 1970s were decades in which urban conservation—ecology with an ideology—had come to the fore, and advocate journalists strongly supported this trend.

Concepts and Strategies of Urban Revitalization

American cities were long the destination for those who sought fortune and fame. Though the city usually came in second to the small town in the contest for "favorite place to live," the city dominated American society. The city was the source of manufactured goods, the center of commerce, the locus of great wealth. The city educated, trained, and transformed rural immigrants into sophisticated members of a growing technological society. It was the wellspring of culture, science, and learning.

In their discussions of the dominance of the city, urban planners, economists, geographers, and sociologists have all drawn our attention to the critical role played by the Central Business District in its economic and social life. This emphasis has provided one working hypothesis for "saving" the cities. The hypothesis is based on the premise that a revitalized urban core will produce a ripple effect from the center outward. This premise was originally deduced from a host of earlier studies that had described urban growth patterns as waves or gradients emanating from the center, providing the energy and direction for urban expansion. Therefore, the argument continued, if the center were renewed through the development of new business and commercial activities and upper-income housing, complementary revitalization would spread outward from the center, repeating the earlier pattern in contemporary form. Investment in the core would stimulate investment in other areas, with the overall result of creating renewed, vital cities. In the process, new jobs for the departed middle classes would be developed, helping to lure them back. The middle classes and the elites would once more be housed in fashionable neighborhoods of the cities. Slum clearance at the centers would make the cities more attractive for living, working, and shopping. Inner city areas would then be able to compete successfully with the suburbs by offering similar amenities in an urban setting, e.g., center city shopping malls with easy parking. The large parking garages in many downtown areas are symbols of this hope.

Many cities have been able to achieve remarkable success in transforming the core, their Central Business Districts, by actions based on this hypothesis—witness the new skylines in Chicago, Pittsburgh, Detroit, New York, and Cleveland. The growth of the core in these cities has also produced a phenomenon found in earlier urban growth—zones of transition (Burgess, 1925; Griffin and Preston, 1966). These zones are created when property owners at the edges of the growing core reduce or eliminate routine maintenance and repair of property with the expectation that new land uses will be created as the core expands, raising property values. If the cores do not expand, however, these zones can deteriorate, as they have in the older cities mentioned above, as well as in others. Since the renewed cores have not stimulated anticipated complementary growth, these zones of transition now extend outward from the center for miles (Suttles, 1984). What is now uncertain about a number of our cities is not what is going to happen to the core: it has been revitalized. The real question is what is going to happen at the edges of the core—in the zones of transition—and in the neighborhoods and communities that fall just beyond its shadows. Lower Manhattan offers an illustrative case study of what can happen when a core is rebuilt but the anticipated adjacent expansion does not occur.

By the middle of the 1970s, older inner cities, both in the United States and in other Western countries, were experiencing yet another change in their residential patterns. This change, termed neighborhood revitalization and gentrification, involves the restoration or renovation of houses in older city neighborhoods by middle class households (Clay, 1977; James, 1977; Lipton, 1977; Sumka, 1978; Hamnett and Williams, 1980; Laska and Spain, 1980). The predictions that old inner cities would become almost exclusively residences for ethnic minorities, the poor, and the elderly appeared not to be holding true. Neighborhoods with architecturally rich housing stock were being discovered by a segment of the affluent middle class, white and black, who were willing to accept the real and imagined discomforts of inner cities in order to enjoy remarkably interesting homes—homes that could be purchased at lower prices than those in the suburbs, but offered larger spaces, better construction, and more interesting design.

Those who were most active in revitalizing these neighborhoods tended to be young, urban professionals—the so-called yuppies, as they came to be known in the 1980s. These middle-class urban settlers had relatively high incomes, were childless, college educated, and employed in professional occupations. The neighborhoods preferred by these "gentrifiers" were clustered near the center of cities, close to the areas employing high-salaried professionals of their ilk. They were within easy reach of the cultural and recreational facilities enjoyed by the more affluent and highly educated. In the wake of the in-migration of these new middle-class households came stores and restaurants that catered to this special population.

Neighborhood revitalization and gentrification raised property values. Both early entrants into these areas and long-term home owners probably made substantial profits if they sold after the neighborhood became fashionable. Often the process was alleged to displace older, lower-income renters, since landlords could realize more money by selling to the gentrifiers (Van Til, 1980; Grier and Grier, 1980; Houstoun and O'Connor, 1980). It is probably equally true that revitalization happened where a slow process of abandonment was already under way—the reason that housing was available at such bargain rates in the first place.

The analysts of the impact of neighborhood revitalization and gentrification vary in their opinions about how this process affected older American inner cities. Perhaps the most cautious analysis is found in the President's Commission for a National Agenda for the Eighties volume, *Urban America in the Eighties:* "Although casual observation indicates that portions of central city neighborhoods are indeed experiencing a great deal of housing stock upgrading and restoration, the evidence is spread so thinly across a number of cities that it defies statistical detection"

(1980:29). The most telling data reported in this volume reveal continued patterns of decline and deterioration in these older inner cities.

But the reliance upon "statistical detection" may well miss the more important point: the major impact of revitalization has been on the attitudes people have toward the future of older cities. Living in an inner city neighborhood apparently is appealing to several segments of the middle class, and finding and restoring aesthetically pleasing houses located in vibrant, closely knit communities may represent an alternative direction for urban social organization.

SoHo shares some similarities with other revitalized areas. First, the revitalization and gentrification process is usually carried out by individuals acting on their own initiative, without government support, and without any guarantees that their efforts will be successful in rejuvenating a deteriorating neighborhood. Those who were the early pioneers in a neighborhood often did not care if it would gentrify, or if their investments were economically prudent. These were the "risk oblivious." The speculators—those who hoped the neighborhood would "change for the better" and that their investments would prove wise—were the "risk takers." And those who waited for the neighborhood to change before they committed themselves to restoring or renovating a property were the "risk averse" (Sumka, 1978:18). The risk oblivious, like the early artist pioneers of SoHo, often created a situation that opened an area to other types of settlers—and often subsequently found themselves being displaced by those who did follow them into these areas (Hudson, 1984).

The displacement of the risk oblivious by risk takers was clearly illustrated in SoHo. The pioneer artists were in no way assured that what they were doing was going to have any long-term payoff. Their objective was not to stake out a new urban neighborhood, but to obtain needed work space and residences. Long-term, complicated leases were not part of the early pattern of loft living in SoHo. There was a great deal of movement from loft space to loft space on the part of the artists. Some of these artists were more like urban gypsies than urban residents, finding a temporary place to park their wagons for a while before moving on. But their pioneering in the loft area led to the transformation of the area, and gave it new life and new symbolic meaning (Stratton, 1977). Once these artist pioneers had settled this urban frontier, it became more attractive for other urban settlers—not necessarily other artists.

There are, however, some obvious differences between the gentrification of residential neighborhoods and the process of loft conversions in SoHo. The possible displacement of an existing residential population was not part of SoHo's pattern. There was no residential population for the initial pioneer artists to displace; the spaces they came to occupy were those left empty by departing businesses. As the process of succession developed, all spaces became more desirable, the number of empty spaces declined, and competition for spaces increased. One result was the displacement of the low-income artists by those willing to pay higher rents for the spaces the artists had converted. Landlords were quite willing to replace one illegal tenant with another if the rent could be raised. Finally, landlords were also willing to cancel the leases of those businesses paying marginal rents when they could be replaced with residential tenants able to pay more.

What the general process of neighborhood revitalization and gentrification did for SoHo, as well as for other industrial areas in Manhattan, was to demonstrate that older inner cities could be attractive to middle-class households. Some of these households became willing to rent spaces in factories—redefined as chic and "trendy" spaces. The conversion or "recycling" of industrial buildings to residential use provided opportunities to put these buildings in a more favorable market position than had been feasible before the process had begun. These recycled buildings were also widely publicized in the media, giving to the process a certain legitimacy, as well as making it fashionable.

Lower Manhattan in the 1950s and 1960s

The design of office buildings after World War II was heavily influenced by the Bauhaus style (Wolfe, 1981). These buildings, with their stark, unadorned facades, rise straight up from the sidewalks. They are often built on large lots, and in New York fit more readily into the grid pattern of midtown than onto Lower Manhattan's small lots on narrow streets. Their large, open floor plans look like those of modern factories. But the production lines in these edifices manipulate symbols, not materials. The flexibility of these layouts, like that of their factory counterparts, made older office buildings obsolete—as obsolete as lofts for manufacturing.

The office building boom after World War II made midtown locations more attractive to commercial developers than Lower Manhattan sites. Assembling sizable parcels of land for large office structures was easier in the larger midtown area than it was in Lower Manhattan, which offered few locations that were appropriate for the grand plazas and dramatic ground vistas that many corporate builders were favoring. Thus, by the early 1950s, the office buildings in the financial district at the tip of Manhattan were losing their ability to keep high-rent tenants. Some prominent firms moved to new locations in midtown; others joined the general exodus from the cities to the campuslike office complexes in the suburbs.

Those corporations that remained because of tradition, location, or investment were worried about these trends. Since millions of dollars were at stake, those committed to Lower Manhattan organized the Downtown-Lower Manhattan Association (DLMA) in 1955. Led by the Chase Manhattan Bank, DLMA was to be the vehicle for mobilizing political and financial support for the revitalization of Lower Manhattan. The actions taken by the Chase Manhattan Bank and the DLMA are examples of how organized groups and actors can influence the process of succession, and are central to the theoretical scheme being presented in this study.

Lower Manhattan land use patterns in the early 1950s can be visualized as a series of tiers. At the base was the financial district, with its well-known silhouette. At the next level, on the West Side just above the financial district, was the Washington Market, the food distribution center of New York, a vast collection of stores, warehouses, and food processing plants. Just east of the beginning of the Washington Market complex were New York City's municipal buildings. Above the municipal buildings on the east was

Chinatown. On the west, above the municipal buildings, and stretching over to the Hudson River, were the beginnings of the loft district that spread up the West Side, crossing Canal Street and reaching Houston Street. The western border of the loft area above Canal Street was Little Italy. The plans for redeveloping Lower Manhattan recognized, implicitly and explicitly, the land use patterns in these different tiers.

In the redevelopment plans, the financial district, rebuilt, was to remain the base. The Washington Market would be razed and relocated at Hunt's Point, in its place, the World Trade Center and new office buildings would be built. Monumental housing developments were planned for the areas of decaying piers along the river. Recreation and entertainment centers would be strategically placed throughout. All would be joined together in a new city within the city. These visions were given form in a massive planning document, *The Lower Manhattan Plan* (Wallace et al., 1966). The plan simply wrote off the existing manufacturing below Houston Street. The proposed elimination of this sector of New York industry was readily accepted by the planners, since the assumption was that these areas were no longer vital to Manhattan's manufacturing future. While there were some provisions made for relocation of existing manufacturing and commercial firms, no one involved in the planning process gave serious thought to helping the old manufacturing and commercial businesses recover or sustain themselves in Lower Manhattan. In the master plan, the area above Canal Street—SoHo—was targeted for new middle-income housing.

In the City Planning Commission's *Plan for New York City* (New York City, 1969), Lower Manhattan was envisioned as a center for international corporate business; housing for the expected labor force was to be built on its fringes, incorporating landfill projects that would replace aging and dilapidated piers no longer used for shipping. Manufacturing in Lower Manhattan was not considered vital enough to merit inclusion in these plans. The Lower Manhattan Expressway project was also under study; it would cut across the city from the Holland Tunnel to the Manhattan Bridge, severing SoHo and Little Italy from downtown.

■ A view of the World Trade Center from the middle of West Broadway. The dramatic contrast highlights the different land-use patterns, and demonstrates why SoHo seemed obsolete for contemporary New York. (Photo courtesy of Melvin Reichler.)

These projects, although tentative, did have some consequences. Owners of buildings threatened with possible condemnation were understandably reluctant to invest in building improvements or maintenance. The area outside the developing blocks took on the appearance of a zone of transition, with the tentativeness that characterizes such areas (Griffin and Preston, 1966).

Like any major development scheme, the Lower Manhattan Plan was composed of several component parts to be phased in over a period of time. The Chase Manhattan Bank, in its role of leader, would build a new office building, a $120 million structure that would revitalize the area and set the tone for redevelopment. The bank also began a massive acquisition program of contemporary art, "not only for the new Chase Manhattan Plaza but for its eight overseas offices. More than 4,700 works of art by 1,500 artists" were purchased through this program (Simpson, 1981:26). Somewhat ironically, this program stimulated the production of art in SoHo, and encouraged artists to locate there at the same time that SoHo was being labeled obsolete as a commercial location.

A second major project in this initial phase of development was the World Trade Center, built on the site that had housed the Washington Market. Wiping out the wholesale food area also destroyed a large number of adjacent businesses that had been dependent on the market and the traffic it generated (Lyon, 1969). The World Trade Center displaced a large blue-collar labor force as well as the stores and services that catered to it. Some of the labor force and businesses did relocate to Hunt's Point; others were dispersed; some businesses closed altogether.

To summarize: beginning in the early 1920s, there was renewed interest in linking art and technology, a linkage that had its foundation in a political ideology that was most clearly reflected in the Bauhaus movement in Germany. The rise of Nazism led to its repression there and, as a consequence, its leaders dispersed to more tolerant countries such as the United States, where it flourished. Politics and art are, of course, never sharply separated: in the 1930s the Communist Party incorporated artists into the Popular Front movement and gave a new social role to, among others,

American artists; at the end of World War II, the government of the United States mounted shows of American abstract art to be sent abroad to demonstrate that our artistic achievements matched our political and economic hegemony.

Art and technology forged new links after World War II, employing some of the most sophisticated advances in technology. This linkage was even institutionalized in 1966 with the establishment of Experiments in Art and Technology, Inc., located in New York City. New technologies demanded new spaces, and some of these were found in the old industrial buildings of Lower Manhattan that provided large inexpensive studios. These industrial lofts also served as illegal residences for working artists who successfully combined work and residence in a way reminiscent of the Bauhaus movement, and in the process created a new artistic community—SoHo—and with it a new area for tourism. The efforts of these artists to build a new community and to produce art found strong support in the media, which discovered a new social role for itself in advocacy journalism.

The discovery of the benefits of living in cities in the 1970s stimulated neighborhood revitalization and gentrification. Urban life became attractive again. Old cities were not destined to be an unpleasant residue of an outmoded past inhabited by the poor, the social inept, and racial minorities, but a vital arena for innovative living, creative life-styles, and new commercial functions.

During the 1960s and 1970s, artistic movements, technological innovations, political action, advocacy journalism, and gentrification swept in on SoHo to create a complex social matrix that transformed this area that had been considered no more than an industrial wasteland into a vibrant new community with a social mission and a political consciousness.

4 ■ Social Dynamics in SoHo: The 1960s and 1970s

Succession in the Postindustrial City

The process of succession can be measured by changes in the size, density, age, and other demographic features of the population; by the number and kinds of social institutions in the area; and by the variety and number of businesses found in communities undergoing succession. But these data cannot be used to assess other social dynamics that occur in communities experiencing succession. Individuals and groups form new relationships, develop social networks, exchange information, compete, and cooperate to create a new community structure and organization. Combining the statistical dimensions of succession with the social psychological dimensions creates the opportunity for a more accurate and complete analysis of the process than either alone can provide.

The strength of human ecology is its ability to analyze succession comparatively by using demographic and other aggregate data for a large number of areas like census tracts. One of its limitations, however, as Hawley has insisted, is that "it is not prepared to provide explanations for all the manifold interactions, criticisms, and collisions that occur within the bounds of a social system" (1968:336). In our study of SoHo, this limitation to understanding can be mitigated by examining some of the social psychological

77

processes that helped shape it, and by focusing on the actors and groups that participated in and influenced the succession process.

Every process of social change creates some measure of uncertainty. In the instance of land conversion, this uncertainty may be only temporary, while owners, renters, investors, and entrepreneurs quickly assess the situation and decide on how to profit from the next most likely and reasonable alternative use for buildings and land undergoing disinvestment, vacancy, or "trouble." When this uncertainty extends over long periods, however, each potential occupant looks to others for ideas on what will happen next. Impatience and anxiety succeed assurance and self-confidence, and traditional risk structures are replaced with experimental ones. The markets are not fixed or predictable, and sudden responses supplant studied adaptations. What seems to work for the moment is accepted on faith, more emotional than rational in its dynamics.

Where this occurs—and it seems increasingly to be the case in our declining cities—land use conversion takes on some of the following features. First, exceptional and highly unorthodox leaders may emerge, presenting astounding, sometimes seemingly utopian proposals for conversion. Second, the debate over conversion may come to include a host of ideological arguments that sometimes have little or nothing to do with assuring the maximum return on land rents, but a great deal to do with broader issues of social justice, public taste, and media visibility. Third, groups which support one or more of these ideological positions may become actively involved in decision making, forcing the issue into the political arena rather than leaving it to the economic logic of the marketplace. Fourth, public officials may inevitably become involved because of the conflicting demands of organized constituencies; organized groups making demands for justice and equity create a political climate in which government indecision becomes a political liability. Fifth, the mass media may help define the issues because the events become news, and the battles involve social issues that the media can champion. Ultimately, these social, political, and economic forces move toward a new equilibrium—and interim experiments become routine solutions. All these features characterized the process of conversion of manufacturing and commercial loft spaces in Lower Manhattan to residential use during the period from 1955 to 1971.

The general uncertainty about the future of Lower Manhattan actually facilitated the subsequent unanticipated development of SoHo. The new office construction in the Wall Street area, including the World Trade Center, did raise land values just outside these immediate neighborhoods. On the other hand, no one could predict just how far the ripple effect of these changes would carry, and whether or not they would reach Canal Street—the southern border of SoHo—or beyond. Zones of transition have usually been described as being in limbo, waiting for the next expansion from the center that will push land values up and displace existing uses and buildings. But if expansion does not occur, a zone of transition can take on semipermanent features, e.g., it can house marginal businesses whose openings and closings can become as routinized as more "stable" operations. In fact, the very fluidity of these areas can give them a cachet that can make them more resistant to change than urban analysts have often assumed. This is not to assert that these operations are not vulnerable to displacement— only that they are more durable than one might anticipate given their transitory appearance. A zone of transition, almost by definition, is a prime target for invasion and subsequent succession. There are expectations on the part of those who hold property in these areas, those who are located there, and those who are looking for land to develop or move into that make these areas ripe for new land use patterns. This was the situation of SoHo at the beginning of the period under study, when the artists began their quiet invasion into SoHo lofts. The few public officials who were aware of this invasion apparently believed that these "transient" artists were simply going to occupy vacant loft spaces during an interim period.

Certainly, the artists were not seen initially by anyone as offering a solution to an urban problem, but simply as a temporary population filling up spaces being abandoned by departing firms. The Artist in Residence Program of the early 1960s did make it legal for artists to inhabit loft spaces, but the artists themselves did not enroll en masse, partly because they could not afford the improvements required to gain legal residential status for their lofts. The artists' reluctance to participate in a program designed for their benefit and protection certainly made public officials question their willingness to be responsible citizens, to meet acceptable standards of conduct as loft tenants. Artists, after all, were a rather unstable lot at best, with little capital or other power to rebuild an urban area. Their activities were not systematic in any obvious way. They were not "developers," only an unorganized body of individuals operating at the margins of society and occupying spaces illegally. They offered nothing in the way of a coherent program with an agenda for urban planning. Ad hoc "renewal" was beyond the imagination of urban planners, land developers, and financial institutions.

When artists moved into SoHo loft spaces, few if any of those responsible for "saving the city" recognized that their individual efforts could significantly change land use patterns. The entire ideology of 1950s urban renewal was based on large-scale development. The illegal conversions of lofts did not have any place on the agenda. City officials could be tolerant of the artists and even offer tacit support in terms of allowing them to continue their residence for a while. Yet no official dreamed that these residents were a wave of the future or that a series of minor alterations could result in a fundamental restructuring of an entire urban area.

From the point of view of the city, what the artists were doing in converting lofts was imaginative, and even important to the city's economy. That contribution to the economy, however, might be quite temporary, considering how rapidly the market for avant-garde art could change. In any case, the artists could not be given the authority to change an urban area; that was the prerogative of city officials, planners, and "serious" investors. As those with "legitimate" authority pondered what to do with the loft areas, the artists continued to convert lofts in SoHo, and began to build a new urban community.

Creating Community in SoHo

The development through individual in-migration of a residential community or neighborhood where none has existed before is a complicated process. Even when there is an existing residential population, definitions of urban neighborhood are hard to establish, as Suzanne Keller (1968) has so carefully pointed out. It may be as difficult for the researcher as it is for a resident to state with any confidence just when a "community" has emerged. Any operational definition of "community" only serves as an approximation around which to organize the data.

For our purposes, SoHo's emergence as a viable and visible community can be dated as occurring between 1963 and 1965. Even by 1960, however, older residents were already talking about how the area had changed (many of them thought for the worse). By that time, the term "SoHo" was widely used to identify the area *south* of *Ho*uston Street and north of Canal Street, bounded on the west by Sixth Avenue and on the east by Little Italy. The cognoscenti of the art world had recognized the loft areas of Lower Manhattan as a fertile source of new artistic work. By 1965, the initial pioneering period when the artists were living illegally and clandestinely in loft buildings had been mythologized. True, most residents were still living in SoHo lofts illegally, but many had become much more open about their residency than were their predecessors.

What happened early in SoHo's history (1955–63) was a three-part process involving the creation of a new role for the area, increased interaction among individual residents, and the development of neighborhood organizations, with each of these elements reenforcing the feeling residents had for the neighborhood. SoHo became a symbol of America's leadership in modern art, manifesting a new life-style whose principal metaphor was the open space of the loft (Eckhardt and Düttman, 1976). Work and residence, which had become separated as the industrial system became more complex, were reunited in SoHo, which became a community unifying work, residence, and ideology. Among SoHo residents, personal relations were directed at unification through mutual support. Tools were lent and labor exchanged in communal efforts to convert raw spaces to habitable environments. The urban wilderness was being settled (Stratton, 1977). Artistic ideas were shared, enhancing the feeling that it was here that what was important was "happening." Nonthreatening criticism was offered and accepted. The testy relationships of the more competitive New York milieux were muted, if not absent. Soon organizations for improving and defending the community grew alongside organizations for solving the marketing problems of artists.

Once developed, the three levels of community gave the inhabitants—as well as their customers, the tourists, and the city officials—a clear sense of SoHo's unique identity. The residents were no longer trying to avoid being discovered—they had developed pride in their part in transforming a decaying industrial area into a vibrant community. They were willing to claim that art and community in New York were alive, well, and prospering. They had demonstrated that an active citizenry could reclaim a dying area without significant assistance from government or foundation monies. Additionally, unlike some government and private developments, the creation of a community in SoHo did not involve razing the buildings that were there. Nor did it seek to displace the viable blue-collar industries that remained. Indeed, part of SoHo ideology was the recognition of hard work in other endeavors as well as art. In fact, the presence of a blue-collar labor force gave SoHo an urban vitality that was absent in more homogeneous areas.

SoHo residents felt that the city should recognize what had been done by the artists and support it through "appropriate" assistance, such as incorporating SoHo into school districts so that residents with children could have access to schools—something that was denied as long as residence in SoHo was illegal. The city government should provide protective zoning to help SoHo preserve itself for what it was, a special neighborhood on a par with the ethnic and racial communities that the city celebrated. The city, however, should not attempt intrusive management of what the community could do for itself.

The early residents' emotional attachments to the area sprang from a number of sources. The hardships encountered and the sweat labor expended in converting raw loft spaces into usable places in which to live and work imbued these spaces with special significance for their occupants. Their efforts were often in jeopardy—on the one hand from the city inspectors who might threaten them with fines and on the other from profit-seeking landlords who could evict them in favor of higher-paying tenants. The constant stress of these conditions took its toll. But the stress itself generated a stubborn commitment to the goal of being able to live and work as one wanted, in a neighborhood that supported one's values, with those who shared one's dreams. Those who struggled for all this knew, as one artist summed it up: "You don't get this kind of life, you earn it" (Millstein, 1962:24).

The folk history of the early days of SoHo is replete with myths and tall tales, especially about how to avoid city inspectors (Simpson, 1981; Hudson, 1982). For instance, one resident, to hide his residential garbage, used a compactor, then wrapped the finished product into a parcel complete with twine and carrying handle. He subsequently deposited it on a subway platform, with good reason to believe it would be stolen. Another carefully clipped his address from all incoming mail before depositing his trash in public receptacles, so that city inspectors who picked through this trash seeking residential addresses could not discover his. False walls were installed to hide bedrooms; trompe l'oeil paintings disguised kitchens. Everyone had a story about a friend who had deceived the inspectors in one clever way or another.

The very hardships of living in an area without the usual urban amenities (e.g., no local grocery stores or municipal trash service) added to a sense of being embattled citizens, and this spirit was shared by later residents through the mythologizing of the traumas of early occupancy in industrial lofts. Out of such experiences, sentiments and images of distinctive identity developed. The following illustrates the emotions and anxieties generated in the struggle to live in SoHo:

The summer of 1968 was a hot one in New York and a frantic one for me. My firstborn, Jeffrey, had been off the umbilical only a few days when my money—all of it—began riding on a wreck of a building on West Broadway. That summer was a time for learning, and there was a lot of learning to do. The building and my potential loft space both looked catastrophic at the moment, and only a lot of information could salvage either one—information on finances and financing, construction laws and materials, zoning and contracts, prices and contractors. All outward signs indicated that the venture was suicidal, and we needed to learn something, anything, to the contrary. (Stratton, 1977:31)

The creation of a unique and vital life-style also contributed to the sentimental attachment to SoHo. The artists moving in brought with them their aspirations for work and community. Such individualized goals were in direct contrast to the anonymity experienced in fragmented urban society and were, therefore, points of pride. SoHo's reported history prior to the zoning change legalizing residential occupancy of loft space is filled with events which promoted a sense of exceptional attachment and distinctive membership.

All these initial sentiments were reinforced through social interaction. Interaction, of course, occurred from the time of the arrival of the first artists. When SoHo was primarily an industrial and manufacturing area, however, the nighttime and weekend population was sparse, and social contacts in SoHo limited. Those who did live there during this early phase quickly identified others who were living there illegally. One working-class bar became a rendezvous for meetings, a place to gossip, to exchange information, and to find mutual support.

The demands of the process of conversion also led to increased interaction. Those who were engaged in converting loft spaces into living areas often cooperated with others: exchanging labor, sharing information, and teaching each other skills to complete the conversion process. They provided each other with information on where to obtain needed supplies, along with names of reliable and sympathetic contractors. The lumber yards in SoHo became focal points of contact for those working on lofts. And in exchanging stories about the hazards of conversions, noramtive values about their collective goals grew. The recognition of mutual aspirations no doubt increased interaction, and did lead to one obvious form of organized action, the joint showing of works.

As the population of SoHo increased during the 1960s, the opportunities for social interaction also increased. The greater the number and variety of social encounters, the more possibilities for new forms of cooperation and social support. As larger numbers of artists settled in SoHo, networks developed among those engaged in particular artistic endeavors which provided opportunities for more specialized support and cooperative ventures.

Out of these informal relationships grew additional formal inter-actions, since residents recognized that their efforts to find some solution to their illegal status required organized action. The artists in SoHo were under a constant threat of being evicted by the city. Whether or not the city would act to enforce the zoning regulations or to raze the area for other land uses was always problematic. The proposed construction of a Lower Manhattan Expressway added to the residents' worries. The perceived threats were quite real, and the uncertainty of SoHo's future created a high degree of tension among SoHo residents. One response to these fears was the establishment of the SoHo Artists Association (SAA) in 1968.[1] This organization served two functions that help inte-grate urban neighborhoods. On the one hand, the establishment of a formal organization to deal with the municipal government identified the community within the larger social system. Its func-tion was to manage what we might call SoHo's foreign relations. On the other hand, the organization provided a means to develop agreement and unity within SoHo. The effects of this dual role are well described by Simpson:

> The community's problems required that its leadership culti-vate sympathetic, knowledgeable, and essentially personal rela-tionships with city planners, lawyers and architects. This put a value on continuity in leadership and a mastery of a large amount of technical and chronological detail. Residents with only a passing interest in the issues could not play a constructive part. Thus those who did pay the price in time and energy to become sufficiently involved—time and energy they felt stolen from their real work, their art—developed a sense of moral righteousness which justified their leadership and its style in their own eyes and in that of most residents. (1981:165)

Still another feature of SoHo's structured development that helped in the creation of a community was the joining of work

place and residence. Indeed, this was one of the major characteristics that made SoHo an attractive area for artists. Being there
twenty-four hours a day made them more accessible to one
another. They worked on kindred tasks, and they mutually supported an aesthetic consensus and a positive attitude about their
chosen work. For avant-garde artists this reassurance helped discount the criticisms that others—whether their families, friends,
other artists, or the public—leveled at them (Becker, 1982, offers
some general principles on how "art worlds" develop).

There is one final dimension to SoHo's organizational development as a community: the establishment of a community press.[2]
The *SoHo Weekly News* began publishing in 1973. In Simpson's
assessment, it "featured the 'outrageous' as a new fashion in
dress, human relations, and recreation—a style which utilized
art-gallery symbolism as a prop for a new conscious life-style"
(1981:228). Its initial editorial policies focused on presenting SoHo
as a unique community with a unique set of problems and issues.
Among its offerings was a nuts-and-bolts column on how to fix up
a loft, with specific instructions on wiring and plumbing. Local
happenings and local gossip were prominently featured. Its emphasis on SoHo's artistic commitments, social values, and shared
struggles helped solidify the belief that there was something philo-
sophically special, even transcendental, about SoHo and SoHo's
life-style.

The process of SoHo's emergence as a community demonstrates
once again how communities gain identity and are held together
(Suttles, 1984). Sentiment, interaction, and organization all played
a part in unifying the community and giving it a clearer identity
among the communities in New York. The special feature of the
population, the preponderance of artists, gave impetus to forms of
cooperation that reflected artistic aspirations and philosophies.
Building a community by converting buildings illegally forged a
special bond among these pioneer artists. But it had its costs in
personal stress and collective uncertainty. Some resolution of this
uncertainty needed to be obtained if the community were to survive for long.

From Community to Polity

The early invasion of lofts by artists in the late 1950s and early 1960s can be seen as an ad hoc solution to the problem artists had in finding adequate work and living space in New York. There was no core set of values that knitted these early loft dwellers together except their commitment to art. Their furtive and secret actions, in fact, kept them separated for a time. Although their actions were clandestine, however, loft living was still a means of meeting the need for working space that spread through the gossip system of New York artists. Various kinds of cooperation among artists developed rapidly as the 1960s progressed, and these various forms of mutual support began to take on the aspects of a budding social movement. To realize SoHo's potential of becoming an artistic community, individuals had to see the need for collective action. The early stage of loft conversions was marked by individuals solving idiosyncratic problems: later there were enough common problems to act as catalysts for organized communal action.

All social movements have an ideological base: a set of beliefs of what ought to be, and a sense of mission. The data cannot be made to substantiate a claim that the first few settlers who worked and lived in Lower Manhattan lofts had a clear sense of common purpose. But as their numbers increased, and as social networks developed, particularly in SoHo, these artists gained a self-consciousness and self-confidence that was to be transformed into a program of collective action. Their self-awareness of a shared fate was strengthened by the emergence of a visionary leader, a phenomenon that often marks the early phase of a social movement.

George Maciunas was that leader. Maciunas was an extraordinarily outrageous artist whose work was "in the dadaist tradition of anarchistic and irreverent art" (Simpson, 1981:155). He was one of the early members of the artistic movement known as Fluxus, which in the early 1960s was centered in SoHo—before it was known as SoHo. Some of the flavor of the movement, as well as of Maciunas's irreverent attitude, can be found in his description of the Fluxus "event": it strives "for the monostructural and nontheatrical qualities of the simple natural event, a game or a gag. It is the fusion of Spike Jones, vaudeville, gag, children's games and Duchamp" (Frank, 1976:175). Maciunas lived and worked in a series of SoHo lofts during the 1960s, pouring out works, projects, and plans, all with the prefix Flux or some variation (Frank, 1976). His impact on SoHo was immense. "When SoHo was a gleam in Chester Rapkin's [1963] eye, George Maciunas staged pageants in its streets, conducted tours through its vacant lots, held banquets in its dives. His collective, Fluxus, was a lofthold word" (Goldstein, 1977:24). But his greatest contribution to SoHo's future was his establishing of the original artists' cooperatives in loft buildings.

No one interviewed in this study characterized Maciunas as charismatic: he was, however, extraordinarily imaginative, vigorously antiestablishment, and thoroughly mischievous in his approach to bureaucracies. He was also dedicated to the task of seeing "all SoHo owned by artists cooperatives, and in the mid-60's he set about implementing his plans" (Goldstein, 1977:24). He wanted to create a whole social system. "Beyond residence and studios, Maciunas hoped to establish collective workshops, food-buying cooperatives, and theatres to link the strength of various media together and bridge the gap between the artist community and the surrounding society" (Simpson, 1981:156). Fluxhouse Cooperatives, Inc. was the organization Maciunas created to pursue his objectives. As president, Maciunas had an organizational base for action. In 1966, he convinced the Kaplan Foundation and the National Foundation for the Arts to give him $20,000 to buy his first building, 80–82 Wooster.

With this first loft launched, Maciunas proceeded to co-op a series of buildings, essentially rolling over the initial capital as he sold shares in subsequent buildings. "Only trouble was, Maciunas never bothered to register his co-ops with the attorney general, and the state slapped him with an injunction in 1970—the same year SoHo was born. But he didn't stop. By 1975 he had organized 15 buildings. His co-ops thrived because they were affordable; Maciunas was the only landlord in SoHo who didn't make a profit" (Goldstein, 1977:24). Jim Stratton, one of the shareholders in a Maciunas cooperative, described him as a "prophet, but not for profit."

The list of those who were Maciunas's "clients" read like a Who's Who of early SoHo: Ornette Coleman, Jonas Mekas, Richard Foreman, Nam June Paik. Everyone who counted, or who wanted to, knew Maciunas. Yoko Ono had him design sculptures for her loft. He was especially instrumental in assisting the establishment of Film Makers' Cinematheque, first a theater and archive for films, then a center for experimental video productions and showing. It was run by Jonas Mekas (Davis, 1977).

Maciunas's persuasiveness must have been impressive. Very rational people seemed to be willing to invest in what at that time was a real gamble. But the price was right—cooperative shares in one building were about $4,500. Maciunas recruited "enough foolhardies for a meeting" to make a presentation. "No, he said, living there was not legal. Yes, there was a bit of a risk to the venture, but there were possible routes to legalizing the neighborhood" (Stratton, 1977:31). The "foolhardies" went forward, and the artist cooperatives of SoHo became a reality within two years. Maciunas now had a committed cohort of activists who shared in his dream of an artists' community.

Maciunas always operated as if everyone he recruited shared his vision, attitudes, and methods. He did not recognize that being unconventional in a conventional world had a price, and that while he was willing to act outside the law, others might not be willing to follow him into outlawry. He assumed he could count on a cadre of followers for his schemes. But those who joined his cooperatives later, as well as some of his earlier supporters, grew weary of his idiosyncracies. Some became so disenchanted that they sued him to recover their investments. He became isolated from the more conservative loft converters, particularly those who were buying whole buildings. By 1975, he was no longer a major force in SoHo, either as an artist or as a leader of the cooperative movement.

Despite the personal and managerial failings of this visionary leader, the artist cooperative movement developed swiftly. In August 1967, the first building, 80–82 Wooster Street, was purchased; in September, the second; in November, the third. In the following spring one more was added, in the summer two more were co-oped, and by October 1968, Maciunas had established seven cooperatives. Sixty-five artists lived in these buildings, which also housed four theaters and one film center—the already mentioned Film Makers' Cinematheque, later called Anthology Film Archives. The purchase price of these buildings totaled $1,021,000. Three were in the same block of West Broadway, and six clustered in the northwest quadrant of SoHo.

The rapid development of these cooperatives and their close proximity to each other served to give the movement a sense of power and unity. A great deal of mutual assistance in the renovations helped build solidarity among cooperative members and enhanced their sense of community. In 1968, representatives from six of these buildings met to form the SoHo Artist Tenant Association. (This organization was pivotal in fighting through the zoning changes of 1971. Its successor, the SoHo Alliance, was still active in the summer of 1985, fighting to protect the artistic communities in Lower Manhattan from becoming yuppie havens.) By 1975, SoHo had achieved the status of a flourishing artistic community with a growing, secure future. But George Maciunas, reflecting on its acknowledged success, said, "I wouldn't want to live there any more" (Goldstein, 1977:14).

By the early 1970s, SoHo's organizations had developed a sophisticated arsenal of political weapons. Their power was demonstrated in 1972, when a proposal was made for a sports center in SoHo. The SoHo Artists Association led the opposition to it. "Throughout the summer [1972] those of us who were still around worked to rally support for the cause. And rally them we did. Our own Downtown Independent Democrats, the neighboring Village Independent Democrats, the Environmental Protection Administration, Congresswoman Bella Abzug among them. By the time of the next meeting [of the Board of Standards and Appeals] we were ready" (SoHo Newsletter no. 30, Oct. 19, 1972, p. 1).

On November 14, 1973, however, the Board of Standards and Appeals "voted to approve developer Charles Low's lovely 20-story sports center, deleting only a single level of parking from Low's plans as a sop to the community" (SoHo Newsletter no. 31, Jan. 13, 1973, p. 1). Low also proposed to open some of the facilities to the local residents, but this, too, was seen as merely a public relations ploy.

The SAA proposed to take their case to court. "Even if we lose the court case, the fight is not over. . . . we will demand that the BSA reconsider its approval and reopen hearings to listen to the evidence it did not consider earlier" (*SoHo Newsletter* no. 31, Jan. 13, 1973, p. 1). These strategies show how confident and skillful SoHo residents had become in their use of political resources to protect their community. In the protracted struggle, the SoHo Artist Association and its various allies fended off the developer, and the sports center proposal was defeated.

At the same time, another group had been watching the developments in SoHo. The neighborhood was not merely a decaying manufacturing area into which artists were now moving; it was also the site of a number of historically significant buildings known for their cast-iron facades and unique method of construction, i.e., the use of prefabricated parts (Gayle and Gillon, 1974). In the late 1960s, the Friends of Cast Iron Architecture had been working vigorously to prevent these buildings from being razed. Their efforts were no doubt aided by the arrival of the artists, who helped give these buildings new economic life. In 1973, the Landmarks Preservation Commission acted to give a large section of SoHo a historic designation. Part of the credit for this can be given to the artist residents, because they had helped call attention to this area by making it "one of the most creative centers of contemporary art in the nation" (Landmarks Preservation Commission, 1973:8).

There is a qualitative difference between the early political agenda of these artists—protecting their right to live and work in lofts—and their later one of purchasing buildings and building a community. The initial plea of the artists was to be left alone, to escape from the harassment of city officials for their illegal occupancy of unused industrial spaces. These artists argued that they were providing new, productive uses for spaces that were no longer being used by the older industries. They were making a positive contribution to New York's economy in producing a marketable product, art.

The creation of artist cooperatives changed the political agenda in the loft areas of Lower Manhattan. The first struggle had been over the right of individual artists to live and work in loft spaces. With the artists' cooperatives acting as an anchor that gave stability to their presence in SoHo, the issue became the defense of a community. The argument was made that if artistic production was to flourish, it needed a community in which to do so: a community that maintained an elan nurturing artistic talent.

While such a community had been developed through the artists' cooperatives on a seemingly sound foundation, its future was not assured. Indeed, it was highly vulnerable. Its vulnerability stemmed from several sources. First, loft living as a life-style had a wider appeal; those attracted to it included a number of affluent nonartists. Their invasion of SoHo could raise the rents of loft spaces and the prices of loft buildings. That would begin to exclude new artists from finding spaces in SoHo and seriously threaten those who were already there. Second, the economic gains that could be made through loft conversions could attract developers who cared little about artists (or art), who could make large profits by wholesale conversions of buildings, and by reducing the size of living spaces to that of more conventional apartments make them unusable—if not too expensive—for artists. Finally, SoHo's potential as a tourist attraction could be equally detrimental to the preservation of the environment. A cheapening and vulgarization of the social milieu would undermine the artistic vitality of SoHo. The precedent of Greenwich Village offered sufficient evidence that an artistic enclave could be turned into a high-priced residential area in some places, and a honky-tonk tourist area in others.[3]

SoHo offered an example of how individuals working together could save a dying area. But once saved, it had to be protected from possible exploitation that would cheapen and ultimately destroy its cultural and social contributions. Loft ownership provided one means for artists to maintain the community. The political power of loft owners became pivotal in the several zoning decisions affecting SoHo in the 1970s.

What had begun as random invasion of empty loft spaces by a few artists had developed into a self-conscious artistic community in SoHo. The succession of loft conversions there also created new ways for artists to secure housing through cooperative efforts, a new area for middle-class housing, a new tourist attraction, and a new urban community. SoHo's success stimulated the search for other lofts that could be converted to residential use in Lower Manhattan.

5 ■ The Expansion of the Loft Conversion Movement

The Initial Expansion of Loft Conversions

The growth of SoHo as a recognized center of artistic production and innovation made it increasingly important to working artists everywhere. It became a place where art was produced and marketed, where styles and trends were discussed, established, and discredited. In the early years (1955–61), the individual artist had worked clandestinely behind locked doors, but as the SoHo artists came to mingle with one another socially and professionally, as their presence came to be known outside the area, as SoHo developed a reputation as the new bohemia, the neighborhood came to resemble Greenwich Village during its several early periods of artistic activity and reputation (Ware, 1963).

Many who are not artists value living in a vibrant, creative community such as SoHo. The presence of working artists, whose productions were being shown in the fashionable galleries and reproduced in the important art magazines, contributed to the elan of the community. Such a milieu attracted prosperous residents who were often more affluent than the pioneer artists. The development of loft living as a life-style increased the attraction of SoHo and other loft areas for those who simply found the social environment agreeable. The growth of a community with social networks and neighboring patterns, as well as smart shops and trendy restaurants, made SoHo a desirable middle-class neighborhood. Loft spaces were sought after not only because they were part of a new chic scene in New York, but also because they were reasonably priced living spaces—in fact, comparative bargains—in the expensive and tight housing market of New York.

The construction of high-rise office buildings that had begun in the 1950s continued into the 1980s with varying degrees of intensity, and resulted in the loss of manufacturing spaces and relatively inexpensive housing in Manhattan and an increase in the demand for luxury apartments by highly paid executives and others. Some housing projects, like the performing artists' apartment building in the west Forties, subsidized middle-class occupations. The decline in manufacturing activities also reduced noise, congestion, and dirt, opening to the middle class attractive neighborhoods that had previously housed only the poor and disadvantaged or industry—often in combination.

Two of the locations that lost manufacturing business adjoined SoHo: NoHo and TriBeCa. NoHo is an acronym for *no*rth of *Ho*uston Street; the area borders SoHo to the northeast. TriBeCa is the *tri*angle of land *be*low *Ca*nal Street that touches the Lower Manhattan Central Business District at its southernmost point; it joins SoHo on the south at Canal Street. While SoHo's eastern boundary is Little Italy, TriBeCa's is Chinatown. As with SoHo, no one is certain of the date of the initial residential conversion in either NoHo or TriBeCa, but conversions in these areas clearly began after SoHo's development was well established. (For more detail on NoHo, see Freiberg, 1975; for TriBeCa, Johnston, 1977). Again, the initial conversions were illegal. The struggle for legal residential status developed more quickly in these two areas, however, because city agencies as well as residents had learned from the SoHo experience how to handle the changing patterns of occupancy with some speed, efficiency, and effectiveness.

In 1976 modifications that recognized the continued decline in manufacturing in Lower Manhattan, as well as the increased possibilities of converting commercial and industrial space to residential use, were made in the zoning laws. The zoning changes were expedited by the government's conclusion that art, an important economic resource for the city, needed space for its production. NoHo was attached to SoHo as a zoning unit, and the ordinances governing both were modified. The size of legal conversions was increased from 3,600 square feet of lot space to 5,000, except for property fronting Broadway—still restricted to 3,600 square feet. Both NoHo and SoHo were to be restricted to artist occupancy—a provision never fully enforced. The ordinances governing TriBeCa were more generous, and placed no restrictions on type of occupant (*Lofts*, 1981:26–27). The zoning changes were important as part of the city's attempt to assert some control over the conversion process, and to regain authority and credibility in land use development. The availability of all three areas as legal locations for loft conversions stimulated the process of loft conversions elsewhere.

Loft Conversions beyond SoHo, NoHo, and TriBeCa

Loft spaces built and used for manufacturing on Manhattan Island stretch from the Lower West Side, outside the financial district, all the way up the West Side to about Fifty-ninth Street (see fig. 2). These are areas that are very specialized with regard to economic activities, reflecting the ecological pattern of clustering. The garment district is one example of this pattern, with its concentration of designers, manufacturers, suppliers, showrooms, and auxiliary services. But there are also the handbag manufacturers' district, centered around the Empire State Building; the graphic arts center, which lies above Canal Street and west of Sixth Avenue; and the meat market at the western end of Fourteenth Street.

The exodus of some of these manufacturers from Manhattan opened up loft buildings throughout the areas below Fifty-ninth Street. Some of these areas have only a few loft buildings, others more: but none have the concentration of SoHo, NoHo, or TriBeCa.

Below Fifty-ninth Street there are sudden transitions from residential to manufacturing to commercial zones, and from residences of the rich to those of the poor. These sharp and abrupt

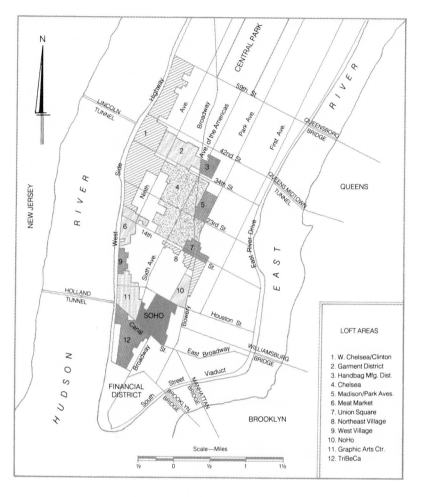

■ Manhattan Loft Areas (Courtesy Keith R. Gentzler)

shifts are easily apparent as one moves through these streets.[1] Loft buildings and other commercial buildings close to "good" areas were especially ripe for conversion, because they could be readily incorporated into established residential neighborhoods that already supported a wide array of stores and services that met residential needs. The zoning maps of New York indicate very clear demarcations between residential and manufacturing areas, but these lines could easily be crossed if enforcement were not vigorously pursued (*Lofts*, 1981).

As in SoHo, the city tolerated illegal conversions in these areas. SoHo, however, had very clear boundaries and a great homogeneity among building types. Its obvious boundaries of wide streets on three sides gave it unit character, and permitted a much more simple zoning solution to the conversion problems. This was true also for NoHo and TriBeCa. Other areas were not as easily distinguishable, and the lack of obvious boundaries posed problems for rezoning (see the zoning maps in *Lofts*, 1981, for details).

SoHo established a precedent for recycling an area that was suffering from economic decline into one with a new economic base—art and tourism—while keeping the older, profitable businesses operating there, and adding housing to the mix. It had done this without government authority or subsidy, although the city actually offered passive support for loft conversions. The city did not enforce the restrictions on loft conversions aggressively or systematically. It did not adhere closely to the requirements of an artistic occupation for the Artist in Residence Program, or artist certification as stipulated in the 1971 zoning ordinances for SoHo. All of this encouraged loft conversions in Lower Manhattan. When the number of lofts in an area like NoHo or TriBeCa became large, the city modified the zoning laws to attempt to exercise some control over the process—but always after the fact. It is little wonder that the attractiveness of loft spaces and the profits to be made encouraged individuals and developers to ignore the city's threat about curbing the spread of loft conversions.

The distribution of the conversions of industrial buildings in Lower Manhattan was analyzed in the 1977 report of the City Planning Commission, in a document appropriately called "Residential Re-Use of Non-Residential Buildings in Manhattan." This report detailed the extent of the dispersion of residential conversions below Fifty-ninth Street. There were 526 conversions reported in eleven identifiable communities outside of SoHo, NoHo, and TriBeCa, and only 47 of these were legal conversions (*Residential Re-Use*, 1977:10–12). The definition of legality used was a certificate of occupancy obtained from the Buildings Department.

These data thus showed that the loft conversion process was occurring just about everywhere there were manufacturing buildings, including the boroughs of Brooklyn, Queens, and the Bronx. While the residential re-use study showed that loft conversions were spreading throughout Lower Manhattan and elsewhere, it also revealed that there were still large numbers of industrial buildings that were not being converted. Even in SoHo, the epicenter, there were a sizable number of buildings with no conversion activity as late as 1984. Other buildings in SoHo were only partially converted. SoHo has remained a viable location for industrial activity, even in the face of constant pressure to expand the residential market, giving some support to Rapkin's 1963 conclusions that viable, profitable manufacturing could be found there and maintained. Manhattan's manufacturing sector is being reduced, but it has not disappeared, and seems able to resist displacement where profit margins are high enough to meet the rent. It can successfully compete against alternative uses, and early fears of its complete elimination appear no longer warranted.

The Patterns of Loft Conversions below Fifty-ninth Street[2]

Below Fifty-ninth Street, there are 1,054 loft buildings in addition to those in SoHo. These buildings range in height from one to forty-three stories. Most (53 percent) are seven stories or less. There are also a large number of twelve-story loft buildings below Fifty-ninth Street (265, or about 18 percent).

In 1974 there were 875 residential telephones listed in 353 loft buildings in Lower Manhattan outside SoHo. By 1980, residential telephones had more than doubled, to 1,881 in 636 buildings. In 1974, the ratio of residential telephones to buildings was 2.48 to 1;

■ A typical street scene in SoHo in the middle 1970s. Note the tall building in the center with its rich architectural detail. (Photo courtesy of Melvin Reichler and Judith Reichler.)

Table 5.1   Distribution of the Number of Floors in Lower Manhattan
Loft Buildings

Floors	Buildings (N = 1504)	Percent
1	1	0.1
2	18	1.2
3	63	4.2
4	168	11.2
5	229	15.2
6	217	14.4
7	101	6.7
8	73	4.9
9	39	2.6
10	63	4.2
11	52	3.5
12	265	17.6
13	12	0.8
14	36	2.4
15–20	132	8.7
21 and over	35	3.2

this had increased to 2.96 to 1 by 1980. As with SoHo, the ratio of residential telephones to buildings increased regularly over time.

The pattern of increasing residential density is also revealed in table 5.3. In 1974, for instance, about 41 percent of the buildings with residential telephones had only one phone, but by 1980 this had decreased to about 36 percent. There was a gradual increase in the number of residential telephones per building as the process developed. Yet by 1980, more than 50 percent of the buildings in Lower Manhattan loft buildings being converted to residential use still had two or fewer residential telephones. Once again, the process of residential conversions appears to have occurred through the action of individuals converting single floors in loft buildings, rather than through the conversion of entire buildings by developers—the same pattern of ecological invasion-succession found in SoHo. There were, however, twenty-nine buildings that had no residential telephones in 1977, but that by 1980 had four or more residential telephones, indicating that some conversions were being undertaken by developers—but scarcely on the scale others (Zukin, 1982:135–40) have claimed.

Table 5.2   Distribution of Residential Telephones in Lower Manhattan Loft Buildings and the Ratio of Telephones to Buildings

Year	Residential Telephones	Buildings with Residential Telephones	Ratio of Telephones to Buildings
1974	875	353	2.48:1
1977	1408	481	2.93:1
1980	1881	636	2.96:1

Table 5.3   Distribution of Residential Telephones in Lower Manhattan Loft Buildings

Number of Telephones	1974 (N=353)	1977 (N=481)	1980 (N=636)
1	41.1%	31.8%	36.5%
2	22.1	24.9	20.4
3	13.9	11.9	13.1
4	8.8	11.6	8.2
5	6.2	6.0	5.0
6	2.8	4.0	5.8
7	4.0	4.6	4.6
8	0.6	3.7	3.5
9	0.3	1.5	3.0
10	0.3	—	—

N = buildings

In Lower Manhattan, the buildings with the smallest floors appeared to be the most likely to be converted: just over 38 percent of all floors in Lower Manhattan loft buildings are 3,000 square feet or less, and over 50 percent of all conversions by 1974 had occurred in buildings with floors of this size. The proportion of conversions in buildings of this floor size declined (48 percent in 1977 and 45 percent in 1980) as the process developed. There was a general trend to larger floor sizes as loft conversion spread. This resulted, in part, from the declining number of smaller buildings available for conversion, as well as from the increasing popularity of loft spaces for residential use with those who could afford more expensive units—an indication of the gentrification in loft conversion.

While the general patterns of loft conversions in SoHo and Lower Manhattan are generally the same, there are also some strik-

*Table 5.4   Distribution of Lower Manhattan Loft Buildings with
Residential Telephones by Floor Size*[1]

Floor Size in Square Feet	1974 (N=353)	1977 (N=481)	1980 (N=636)	All Buildings (N=1470)
Under 1000	15.3%	13.3%	12.1%	10.5%
1000–1999	23.5	23.7	21.9	19.1
2000–2999	11.9	11.4	11.0	8.9
3000–3999	13.9	15.8	17.0	15.8
4000–4999	7.9	8.9	9.6	9.2
5000–5999	3.4	4.8	5.8	6.8
6000–6999	4.5	4.8	6.3	6.6
7000–7999	3.4	2.9	3.0	3.4
8000–8999	2.5	3.1	2.5	3.5
9000–10,999	2.5	2.3	2.5	4.1
11,000–14,999	5.7	5.2	4.4	5.9
15,000–19,999	2.5	1.9	1.9	2.9
20,000 and over	2.8	1.9	2.0	3.2
Median Size	3471	3674	3784	4316

N = buildings
[1] There were 34 buildings for which floor size could not be obtained.

ing differences, reflected first in the assessed values of floors and buildings being converted.

The pattern of invasion-succession in Lower Manhattan follows the pattern of SoHo in terms of assessed building values: conversions began in the buildings with the lowest assessed values. However, the 1973 assessments of Lower Manhattan buildings were much higher than those in SoHo. There appears to have been greater resistance in Lower Manhattan than in SoHo to loft conversions in the highest ranges of assessed values, because the higher prices in the former area inhibited any potential developers or residents. In 1974, about 55 percent of the conversions outside of SoHo had taken place in buildings assessed at $25,000 or less per floor. The proportion increased to 58 percent in 1977 and remained the same in 1980. This pattern is slightly different from SoHo's, where invasion of loft conversions moved continuously into higher assessed buildings.

The median assessed value of a SoHo loft building undergoing residential conversion never topped $65,000, while the median

Table 5.5   Distribution of Lower Manhattan Loft Buildings with
Residential Telephones by 1973 Assessed Value of a Building[1]

Assessed Value in Dollars	1974 (N=371)	1977 (N=432)	1980 (N=584)	All Buildings (N=1374)
Under 5999	0.3%	0.2%	0.2%	0.2%
6000–6999	0.9	0.9	0.7	0.5
7000–7999	1.9	1.9	1.4	0.9
8000–8999	2.2	2.3	1.5	1.5
9000–9999	1.9	2.5	2.2	1.5
10,000–10,999	5.4	5.1	3.8	2.5
11,000–14,999	19.6	19.0	17.0	12.6
15,000–19,999	11.4	14.4	17.3	12.3
20,000–24,999	11.0	12.0	13.4	11.9
25,000–29,999	7.3	7.4	8.0	8.4
30,000–34,999	6.9	6.9	6.0	7.4
35,000–39,999	5.0	5.1	5.1	6.3
40,000–44,999	2.8	2.3	3.1	4.1
45,000–49,999	2.5	2.8	2.9	3.8
50,000 and over	20.8	17.1	17.5	25.9
Median Value	159,937	159,850	179,805	

N = buildings
[1] There were 130 buildings for which assessed value was missing.

assessed value of a Lower Manhattan loft building was at least
$160,000 in any year for which data were available. This difference
in assessed values was repeated for individual floors. There were
too few floors in Lower Manhattan loft buildings assessed at
$4,000 or less to be included in the tables; but in SoHo, 2.5 percent
of all buildings had this low an assessment. There was also a
marked difference in the proportion of conversions in buildings
assessed at over $25,000 per floor. In SoHo, only 5.8 percent of the
conversions were in floors over that figure, while in Lower Manhattan 42.6 percent of the floors were assessed this high or higher.

SoHo buildings show a much greater density of conversions than
the buildings of Lower Manhattan. In 1977, the ratio between residential telephones and buildings in SoHo was 4.08:1, while in
Lower Manhattan it was only 2.96:1 in 1980. By 1977, almost
35 percent of SoHo buildings with residential telephones had five
or more, while in Lower Manhattan only 22 percent had this

number in 1980. Finally, 55 percent of all SoHo loft buildings had experienced some residential conversion by 1977, whereas only 42 percent of the loft buildings in Lower Manhattan had.

In the 1970s, loft conversions moved beyond SoHo in ever increasing numbers. While there had been artists converting lofts throughout Lower Manhattan since the process first began, the numbers had been limited: SoHo represented the area with the highest concentration of loft converting artists. The areas immediately adjacent to SoHo—NoHo and TriBeCa—were the first areas outside SoHo to repeat its pattern to an extent that demanded effective city action to address the problems connected with the process.

The loft conversion movement continued to spread all across Lower Manhattan, to any area that had buildings that could be converted. The kinds of profits that could be made encouraged professional developers to enter the market, changing the character of the conversion process. As the expansions progressed, the prices of lofts and loft buildings began to move sharply upward, and viable businesses began to be displaced—increasing the concern of city officials who were responsible for economic planning.

Almost all these conversions remained illegal. The city began to lose its ability to control land use patterns through its various agencies. The still viable manufacturing sector of New York's economy was threatened by indiscriminate replacement if "pure" market forces were permitted to function. Rational planning for housing and the future development of the city was clearly being jeopardized. If the city was to regain its hegemony over land use developments, or at least its traditional power to influence the patterns of change, it had to reestablish its ability to control what was happening. The means the city had at its disposal was zoning: a zoning policy that could assimilate what had already happened and guide future development. The ways in which the city reacted and the politics of accommodation to loft conversions were not simply a political response: these problems were rooted in the city's ecological system, and a full understanding of what heppened requires an interpretation based on human ecological theory.

6 ■ The Political Response to Loft Conversions in Lower Manhattan

The City's Dilemma

In the late 1970s, New York City's government was faced with a dilemma. On the one hand, private individuals, groups, and developers had created new middle-class housing and vital neighborhoods by salvaging industrial buildings that some city planners had written off as obsolete. New businesses, based on art and tourism, were flourishing in areas that had been regarded for some time as economic liabilities to the city. Important historical buildings had been recognized, protected, and preserved from possible destruction. The residents of these areas had become politically powerful, and gained wide support from other interest groups, some politicians, and the mass media. Finally, national publicity had made these areas famous—models for other cities to emulate.

On the other hand, city officials could not claim credit for these positive changes; the process of loft conversions that had made them possible was primarily illegal. Succession in the loft areas was now threatening economically important business centers (Tobier, 1981:39–41). Responsible city agencies had exercised little or no control over the situation. All of this was embarrassing, as well as unacceptable, to the city. There was pressure on city agencies to respond to what was going on in order to reestablish their authority over land use. A major policy reformulation was required: one that would take into account what had happened, what was happening, and what should happen in the immediate future.

The dilemma the city government confronted was complicated because others had taken the initiative in shaping Lower Manhattan's land use patterns, and the city was an awkward latecomer. The tenants who had converted loft spaces, the landlords who were renting them to residential tenants, the developers who were converting whole buildings, and the businesses that were being displaced by these conversions had adapted to changes in Lower Manhattan. Unions with shrinking memberships, wholesalers, suppliers, real estate agents, banks, and other lending institutions had also altered their behavior to accommodate to the changing labor and commercial market. Indeed, most of these groups were ready for yet more loft conversions.

The ability of these groups and organizations to adapt more rapidly than the city stemmed from their comparative flexibility. Municipal governments are not designed to react swiftly to social change (Hawley, 1950:229; 1971:98). Their rate of response is often slowed by the diffusion of power within city government, as well as within the system of which it is a part (Hawley, 1963). A city government is not a "command organization," and usually has to mobilize various constituencies, while placating others, to achieve some kind of effective adaptation to change. Under such conditions, political action may be started at different places in the political structure, depending upon the issues involved.

New York suffers, as David Rogers (1978) has noted, from a very diffuse power base. The sheer size of the city, with its cadres of competing organizations and interest groups, makes political mobilization very difficult. The data Rogers offers complement that of Sayre and Kaufman (1960), who also argue that New York is especially unwieldy because of the lack of concentration of elites.

Nevertheless, by the late 1970s, various agencies (in particular the City Planning Commission, the Office of Economic Development, and the Department of Housing Preservation and Development) realized that something had to be done to address the new conditions that loft conversions had created. To reassert the authority of city agencies over their respective bureaucratic domains, they had to acknowledge, once again, that they were responsible for protecting the residents of the city from unnecessary risks; that they should exercise positive influence over the city's development; and that their political power to exert such influence must not be diminished. The most obvious avenue open to accomplish these goals was to rework the zoning codes.

Developing New Land Use Strategies for Postindustrial New York

The process of changing the zoning ordinances in New York City involved a highly complex set of interchanges, bargains, and deals. Ballinson summarizes this complexity:

> Numerous city agencies had jurisdiction over interests in various aspects of a policy. Among the principal agencies, the City Planning Commission (CPC) had jurisdiction over land use policies, the Mayor's Office of Economic Development (OED) with the plight of industry, and the Department of Housing Preservation and Development (HPD) with the creation of safe, habitable housing. Topping off a very complex recipe for political turmoil was the existence of numerous outside interest groups which were vitally concerned with how the city would react to loft conversions. (1981:55–56)

The city agencies had to deal with problems that cut across their jurisdictions. These problems dealt with art and artists, the enforcement of codes applicable to housing and industry, the protection of industrial spaces, and the future status of loft conversions; they seemed to have no simple solutions.

Consider, first, the issues involving art and artists. The upward trend of loft rents and prices was adversely affecting part of the artistic community. Some artist pioneers who did not own the buildings they lived in were now being displaced. The agencies which had recognized their contribution were confounded as to how to keep these artists in New York City, as well as how to maintain entry level spaces for those trying to establish themselves. In the early 1960s, no one would have predicted that artists could be priced out of loft spaces, and that a new industry—art production—might be jeopardized by subsequent changes in the loft areas.

Second, the illegal conversions had created a large number of residential units that did not meet the code requirements for housing. The creation of a new housing market outside the legal boundaries was a political embarrassment for city officials as well as a geniune concern for those responsible for public safety. This issue was addressed sharply in the New York City Planning Commission's report, *Lofts: Balancing the Equities:* "the safety and continued occupancy of illegal residential tenants is jeopardized by living outside the framework of residential and building law protection" (*Lofts,* 1981:1).

Third, the unanticipated displacement of commercial and industrial activities had also become a serious problem. Various agencies in the city had learned through their own research that economically important manufacturers were indeed being displaced. Primary among these agencies was the Office of Economic Development, which assigned substantial staff time to investigating this problem in 1980.[1] While the exact extent of displacement remained open to question, there was no doubt that some was occurring, and that, without a protective policy, it would increase. Developing policy in this area, however, demanded documentation, which was difficult after a long period of ignoring the issue. No records or assessments of displacement had been made until 1975, and at first these were more impressionistic than systematic.

Finally, there was the realistic anticipation that loft conversions were going to continue. The pressures on the housing market in New York are such that alternatives, in whatever form, have always been pursued by those in need of housing. It was also generally accepted that manufacturing might decline even further, although it would not totally disappear. The issue was how to handle the process of change in ways that were least disruptive to the housing market and the businesses affected.

On one level, then, the question was how to handle the changes that had been and were taking place; on another, it was how to prepare for future changes that could not be specifically predicted. Simply permitting market forces to operate autonomously did not make sense in a city that in so many other areas had effectively employed elaborate planning procedures. If nothing else, it would lead to the appearance of inconsistency and unfairness. Shifts in population, the occupational structure, patterns of residential use, educational needs, and a host of other factors had always been included in these planning efforts; the consequences of particular changes were constantly being evaluated, and were central to the rationale that justified the actions of planners and politicians.

Slowly, city agencies recognized the scale of the loft conversion problem, and placed the following list of issues on their agenda:

1. The zoning laws themselves needed to be changed.
2. Protection for residents had to be assessed.
3. A strategy for relocating displaced manufacturers had to be developed.
4. Some alterations in the current tax abatement policies with regard to renovations of buildings had to be made.
5. The practicality of enforcing any ordinance had to be considered.
6. Finally, the package had to be maneuvered through the political thicket.

These city agencies not only had to deal with each other in reaching a consensus on new policies, but also needed to take into account a wider political structure containing active groups and organizations with their own agendas. As itemized by the City Planning Commission (Lofts, 1981:33–34), groups that became involved in the political process to identify and solve the problems of loft conversions included:

> Community Boards Numbers 1–6
> Housing Committee of the City Council
> Citizens Housing and Planning Council
> The Real Estate Board of New York
> Lower Manhattan Loft Tenants
> International Ladies Garment Workers Union
> United Hatters, Cap, and Millinery Union

The Printing Industries of New York
Counsel for Meat Market Firms
New York Chamber of Commerce
Chambers-Canal Civic Organization
Horatio Street Block Association
Flatiron Association
Board of Standards and Appeals
Office of Economic Development
Department of Cultural Affairs
Department of Housing Preservation and Development

And this list does not contain the critical political body that has the authority to make the final decision needed to carry out a major policy reform—the New York state legislature.

The complexity of the problem can be perceived in the following outline of the diverse agendas of a number of the groups concerned: The City Planning Commission (CPC) wanted to maintain its hegemony over land use policies; the Office of Economic Development (OED) was chiefly concerned about the integrity of the industrial base of New York City; the Department of Housing Preservation and Development (HPD) was interested in the development of safe, habitable housing; the community boards were focused on the viability of the neighborhoods; some unions, like the industrial ones, wanted job protection, while others, like those representing the building trades, wanted work; the real estate industry was interested in how it could profit in a period of changing land use patterns; the artist tenants of lofts wanted protection of their living/work spaces; manufacturers wanted to continue operating; and everyone wanted to have some kind of stability in an unstable system.

In proposing a set of recommendations for the solution of the complex problem, the chairman of the New York City Planning Commission stated the case succinctly:

It asks something of everyone. From developers it asks relocation benefits for displaced business tenants; from industry it asks an orderly transition to residential use in areas no longer recognized as prime business districts; from residential tenants it asks acceptance of regularized safety and housing quality standards; and from the City it demands an investment of law enforcement to assure realization of the twin goals of industrial protection and residential security. (*Lofts*, 1981, Preface)

Before the solution to which the chairman referred was produced, and its zoning recommendations passed by the state legislature, the problems posed by illegal and legal loft conversions had been studied, documented, restudied, and debated; recommendations had been considered, rejected, reconsidered; formal and informal groups had met to achieve a working political consensus on the new policies needed to bring order to an unacceptable situation for the city's various agencies and the groups and organizations affected by the loft conversion process.

The City Planning Commission played a central role throughout the multiple deliberations over loft conversion policies. Its position was critical because it had the authority to make zoning recommendations to the state legislature. Perhaps even more crucial was its preparation of the key documents tracing out the development and ramifications of loft conversions in New York City: *Residential Re-Use of Non-Residential Buildings in Manhattan* (1977); *Action Plan: Report of Mayor's Task Force on Loft Conversions* (1978); and *Manhattan Loft Rezoning Proposal* (1980). The process by which the zoning recommendations were made to the legislature began in 1977, when, in addition to the review and extension of the J-51 amendment,[2] the City Planning Commission made the first systematic attempt (*Residential Re-Use*) to assess the dimensions of the loft conversion process. This study was well documented, but did not result in any immediate action. Illegal and legal conversions continued, as did the calls for action. Both the City Planning Commission and the Office of Economic Development were now experiencing growing difficulties in their ability to carry out their mandates. The Board of Standards and Appeal had the authority to override zoning ordinances, and the frequency of these decisions to override jeopardized the planning process (Ballinson, 1981:64 ff.). By March 1978, the issue had reached the mayor, who, as administrators often do in such cases, created a study group (Task Force on Loft Conversions). It contained representatives from CPC, OED, HPD, the Department of Buildings, and the BSA. Its report, *Action Plan* (1978), was a simple restatement of the problem, with a set of recommendations that were ignored by the mayor's office. The task force then faded away, the push for changes diminished.

Then, in the City Planning Commission's Manhattan office, two planners who had been concerned about loft conversions since their emergency in SoHo (one had been the city's liaison officer to the SoHo Community Board) took the initiative of drafting a report with recommendations. The *Manhattan Loft Rezoning Proposal* (1980) was more complete and more ambitious than the earlier *Action Plan*. But this report also might have been filed away if an incident had not occurred which highlighted the failings of the existing policies.

There are many landmark buildings in New York City that have both historical and aesthetic interest: the Singer Building is one (see Toll, 1969, for comments on this building). When an application for a variance to permit its residential conversion was made to the Board of Standards and Appeals, a number of well-placed city officials opposed granting it, but to no avail. Confronted by their impotence to prevent this particular conversion, city officials mobilized to develop new legislation that would correct the existing power imbalance. The result was the organized review for the rezoning proposals for the loft areas in Manhattan.

Unlike the formal mechanism of the "task force," the process that occurred after the publication of the *Manhattan Loft Rezoning Proposal* was informal and casual. Meeting at lunch and often after normal working hours at their various offices, those concerned agreed that some policy needed to be made with regard to loft conversions. While there was consensus on the need for new policy and the elimination of current practices, the participants were often primarily eager to promote their own agencies' interests; by 1980, however, they were all concerned enough about the general problems to compromise to achieve a consensus solution. Several agencies had begun to prepare position papers on different aspects of how the conversion process was affecting their opera-

■ The famous Singer Building at 561–563 Broadway adds a turn-of-the-century look
to SoHo's architecture, and features such new innovations as fireproofing. Its
delicate iron work and traceried balustrades are definitely Art Nouveau.
A requested zoning variance for this building figured prominently in the debates
over the 1980 zoning changes. (Photo courtesy of the New York Landmarks
Preservation Commission.)

tions. The Office of Economic Development, for example, was interested in assessing just how extensive manufacturing displacement had become—the data reported in Chapter 5 were gathered by OED for this purpose.

There were two primary issues to be resolved politically. The first issue was establishing where residential loft conversions could continue to take place and where they could not. A major consideration in resolving this issue was the protection of manufacturing and associated jobs. Another was the assumption that space in Manhattan needed to be maintained for "incubator industries," especially those that required inexpensive space to test out new ideas and products. The mortality rate among such businesses is high: but, so the argument runs, if one succeeds, the rewards are great. A third assumption was that even if manufacturing was on its way out, its decline and demise was best controlled by permitting a gradual erosion so that other accommodations could be made, e.g., developing industrial areas in other boroughs, retraining workers for new jobs, and planning the economy of Manhattan with more rationality than reliance on market forces alone would permit. Added to this last point was the additional consideration that certain industries needed access to specialized services to survive and prosper.

The second issue needing political resolution was how to manage conversions. Loft conversions, even when illegal, had become a new source of housing in an area of the city that had a chronic housing shortage. The strategies for conversion management had not only to correct previous oversights in housing code enforcements, but also to assure that future conversions would meet the housing code ordinances, and to include loft conversions in the general planning policies for housing in the city.

When all these issues were sorted out, and when a good deal of solid research had verified the extent of the problems, the various participants were in a position to develop a strategy for action. The final details reflected careful bargaining for acceptable compromises. No one group or agency obtained all its original objectives in these negotiations, but the agreements reached created a united front to present the zoning recommendations to the state legislature.

Compromise and the New Political Equation

The various participants summarized their position on the new zoning proposal in the following statement:

> These land use regulations are designed to ensure that adequate industrial loft space is retained for New York City's Manhattan based garment, meat and printing firms. These changes also provide continued and expanded opportunities to create habitable, legal housing in recycled buildings. Recycling is channeled to neighborhoods where residential use is appropriate and where conversion has minimal impact on industrial users. (*Lofts,* 1981:2)

To achieve these goals, the zoning proposal had several components: policies for stabilizing the spaces for businesses; regulations covering loft conversions; and provisions for correcting existing housing code violations in lofts that had been illegally converted. The proposed zones reduced the manufacturing space protected in the Manhattan central business area from 97.7 million square feet to 90.4 million square feet. This opened 7.3 million square feet to residential use for possible loft conversions.

The spaces available for conversion were not evenly spread throughout the area below Fifty-ninth Street. The garment center, northeast Chelsea, the meat market, and the graphic arts center were almost entirely protected. There could be no new residential buildings constructed, nor any conversions, within these zones. The use of J–51 provisions, Section 421 of the Real Property Tax Law (see Ford, 1978: Chapter, 2, for details), and other tax abatement programs was prohibited in these districts. All existing conversons were "grandfathered." (Grandfathering is "a zoning technique which permits certain illegal residential loft tenants to become legal nonconforming users in a particular district." See *Lofts,* 1981:150–51.) No areas were designated for exclusive residential use.

In addition to the exclusion of some manufacturing districts from residential conversion, a second zoning category was developed for mixed use districts which contained a unique provision to help sustain businesses in New York. If a developer wanted to convert a commercial building to residences in a mixed use zone, he or she had to preserve an equal amount of floor space for commercial use, either in the same building or in a comparable building in the same district. Comparability was clearly specified, to insure that the preserved space was suitable to manufacturing (*Lofts*, 1981:73–83). Such space would be "deeded," that is, made part of the permanent record of a particular building. A further protection of commercial spaces was provided in a provision which granted a new three-year lease with a two-year renewal option to any manufacturing or commercial firm that had been a tenant for at least two years.

Recognizing that some commercial tenants were likely to be displaced even under the new zoning code, a further provision was included to help displaced firms relocate in New York, assessing the developer a fee for space converted ($9.00 per square foot). The fee was indexed for inflation, and paid into the Industrial Relocation Fund, to be administered by the Business Relocation Assistance Corporation. There were subtle variations built into this procedure: e.g., if the developer assisted displaced tenants to relocate in New York, the fee would be adjusted (*Lofts*, 1981: 93–105). This made residential developers part of the strategy to protect business (Hornick, 1982).

These provisions provided protection for manufacturing areas in New York. But the problems involving existing illegal conversions remained. In almost every instance, illegal loft conversions did not meet code requirements for residential dwellings. Under the new zoning code, these violations were to be corrected by vigorous city actions that would make lofts meet the requirements for a certificate of occupancy. As the introduction to these new provisions argued, "Enforcement efforts of housing code ordinances, which relied on voluntary compliance, were ineffectual. This policy of neglect has not been benign. Loft tenants, both residential and industrial, have suffered" (*Lofts*, 1981:55). The standards for residential conversions included a number of specific provisions, net impact of which was to increase conversion cost; thus probably to increase the gentrification of some converted lofts, encourage developers to cut up loft areas to maximize profits, raise the prices of "grandfathered" lofts, and make it difficult for a solo converting artist to find an affordable loft—all of which contributed to stabilizing and institutionalizing the loft conversions in Lower Manhattan to a degree that no previous actions had been able to accomplish.

Buildings in the manufacturing districts (M1–5A and M1–5B) could be converted legally to joint living/work quarters, with, of course, restrictions. First, the lot coverage of the buildings could not exceed 5,000 square feet (in actuality, lot coverage and floor size were almost identical). This restriction was tightened to 3,600 square feet on buildings fronting Broadway—the importance of the Broadway corridor for manufacturing was given high priority and therefore greater protection. "However, such quarters may also be located in a *building* occupying more than 5,000 square feet of *lot area* if the entire *building* was held in cooperative ownership by artists on September 15, 1970" (*Lofts*, 1981:119). Protection was provided for those artists who had become established and theoretically had invested their money in loft conversions. There was an additional provision that permitted a current occupant who did not meet the qualifications for an artist as defined by the Department of Cultural Affairs to remain as a resident in the M1–5B districts. But his or her right of occupancy was non-transferable, and would cease immediately "upon the vacating of the space" (*Lofts*, 1981:119).

The remaining details of the 1981 zoning proposals addressed several other problems associated with legal conversions. For example, since it was possible to mix preserved space and converted space in the same building, residential units could be "sandwiched" between two manufacturing floors. Sandwiching had taken place during illegal conversions, and these spaces were exempted from the zoning prohibitions. The argument was that landlords could evict existing manufacturers from spaces over residential ones if prohibitions against sandwiching were totally enforced. "The Commission recognized 'sandwiching' as an imperfect alternative, but the only solution which avoids these undesirable consequences" (*Lofts*, 1981:44).

These zoning codes were essentially designed to halt illegal conversions; to give the city a chance to stabilize conditions; and to introduce more rational, if more bureaucratic, procedures. They took into account some of the unintended results of the city's earlier policies and practices. For manufacturers and their landlords, the codes affirmed the city's commitment to support manufacturing for the immediate future. For artists, residents, and developers, they clarified the policies for housing and conversions. All those affected by the new zoning codes recognized that subsequent changes in the national or local economy might necessitate additional modifications. But for the moment, a new equilibrium had been established.

One problem remained: halting illegal conversions and legalizing illegal residential lofts. The zoning amendments simply outlined where and how additional conversions could occur. To prohibit continued illegal invasion, the Office of Loft Enforcement was created to insure that no new illegal conversions would be undertaken. Its structure gave it a quick and effective means of halting the process of conversions (Weisbrod, 1981). The other side of the problem was bringing illegal dwelling units located in lofts up to housing code standards as detailed in the zoning ordinances just reviewed and other applicable laws. The responsibility was given to the Department of Housing Preservation and Development. The two issues that needed resolution were how to obtain a certificate of occupancy for converted lofts and how to guarantee the current tenants the protection provided to other tenants in New York City housing.

Put somewhat differently, the questions were two. Who pays for the legalization process—tenants or landlords—or is it split? And what is going to happen to rents when dwelling units are legalized? The problem for HPD was extraordinarily complicated, because the number of dwelling units was unknown—20,000 residents in 10,000 units covering 15 million square feet was one estimate (Ballinson, 1981:133). The range of rents and their distribution was equally unknown. These issues had not been effectively dealt with by the time this research had been completed.

7 ■ Conclusion and Implications

Equilibrium in the Loft Areas

Invasion-succession is a process that occurs within the context of larger patterns of social change: it is not self-generating, but an adaptation to environmental conditions that are created by exogenous and/or endogenous forces. The invasion of the lofts of Lower Manhattan by pioneer artists during the period under consideration is an example of this process. In the process of succession that followed the initial invasion, the new population altered the land use patterns and social fabric of the area in such a way as to open the possibilities for subsequent succession and adaptation.

Although it is difficult to specify when a process of succession ends, the direction it takes, according to ecological theory, is toward a new equilibrium. Complex social systems appear to be undergoing constant change when viewed from a broad historical perspective: closer examination, however, usually reveals periods of equilibrium within the process that have been maintained for some time (Rostow, 1966, offers such an interpretation for national economies). These periods are attributable to two primary sets of causes. Equilibrium can result from the action of social forces beyond the control of human actors as well as from the conscious efforts of social actors—although the actual outcome may never match what the conscious actors desired or planned (Merton, 1937). In modern complex societies, these processes generally operate simultaneously (Gamson, 1968:185–94).

Most of the early loft conversions were carried out without much planning, and with little intent on the part of the pioneer artists to change Lower Manhattan in any way. As the population of pioneer artists increased, however, a process of succession began that did result in major changes. Various social actors began to see new possibilities and opportunities arising from the initial pioneer invasion. These actors became more conscious of the actions they were taking, and they sought ways to influence the patterns of succession and create equilibrium.

The initial invasion of a few pioneer artists might have made little difference to the future of Lower Manhattan if their numbers had remained small and their occupancy had been only temporary. But their numbers increased, and their presence and the changes it produced triggered subsequent developments that were anticipated by neither themselves nor the city government. This process of adaptation had certain features that began to pose serious problems for the city. Primary among these problems were the illegal status of the residential occupants, the displacement of businesses, and the dangers inherent in these conditions.

There are a number of ways social systems can reduce or eliminate instability and disequilibrium and attempt to establish order, routine, and balance. For example, when confronted with unrestrained competition, business firms can form cartels; guilds and unions can restrict the numbers entering a given occupation, trade, or profession; and governments can apply a wide range of powers to maintain order. This study of loft areas in New York City demonstrates that human ecology includes these conscious attempts, as well as those conditions that lie beyond the control of a social system, in its explanation of how social systems move toward equilibrium.

It might have been anticipated that the residential conversion of lofts would have been more extensive than the data in Chapters 2 and 5 indicate. After all, there were two conditions which would encourage such an activity: (1) loft spaces were real bargains in the Manhattan housing market, and loft living was demonstrably an attractive, even exciting, choice for those who wanted to enjoy the latest fashion in urban housing; and (2) there appeared to be a consistent trend on the part of manufacturing and some commercial businesses to leave the city—indeed, some businesses were even being displaced by conversion activity. But the process of loft conversion in Lower Manhattan actually slowed down in the late 1970s: there were only, after all, a finite number of loft buildings to convert; the drawbacks of living in converted industrial space and the problems involved in making them comfortable residential spaces became increasingly apparent; the remaining manufacturing and commercial firms became protected from displacement by developers and others; and the cost for loft spaces dramatically increased.

Leaving aside the most obvious limitation on loft conversions—the finite number of lofts in Lower Manhattan—those who saw loft conversion as a solution to their search for ample residential space at a good price in Manhattan began to realize that such conversions had serious drawbacks, and that realization had a significant influence on limiting the movement. Artists had made loft living look romantic. They had done the same thing for garrets, but few of us really find a garret the place to live the good life. Books and articles were published that indicated just what the loft converter might encounter: "Crud. Garbage. Piles of drek, dross, dung. No less than a half century of it sits staring from every corner, saturating bricks and flooring, oozing out of the old pipes. Often it rises from the shadows in the form of walls, machinery, shelving, rag bales—all of which must be disposed of in some way before the loft dweller can even think about the real problems of conversion to a residential space" (Stratton, 1977:112). And the author of these words, beside being a veteran of zoning battles to protect the integrity of the artistic communities in Lower Manhattan as well as a skilled and competent craftsman, is an enthusiastic loft converter who has undertaken the process more than once.

Even in those articles that presented loft living as a wonderful new world for the affluent middle class, in which four-color photographs presented lofts as dramatic spaces for gracious living, the warnings were not muted: "Unless someone has already done the preliminaries in your loft, you'll have to hack out your home from the urban wilderness. You may be faced with 50 years' worth of leather scraps, paper shreddings or paint chips. . . . There is no point in trying to live a floor above a factory that sends asbestos dust through the vent onto your eggs" (Hellman, 1977:63). Such articles also warned that there were building codes and restrictions on residential development—the tolerance for artists that the city had shown in the early days of their illegal conversions was no longer being extended. At a minimum these caveats introduced a sobering effect on those who were seeking lofts to convert and they came about at the same time that the city, having second thoughts about the displacement of manufacturing tenants from Lower Manhattan, was taking action to control the process more effectively through new zoning regulations.

The initial residential migration into SoHo, NoHo, and TriBeCa was made possible because of the exodus of many businesses from these areas. The increasing importance of art as an industry justified the tolerance city officials had shown to illegal conversions by artists: but when the sole purpose for conversion became residential and developers began to play a significant role in the process, the city had to reconsider its policies. A critical issue became: were the increasing loft conversions simply filling empty spaces no longer needed by departing businesses, or were they displacing businesses employing a large number of blue-collar workers and quite able to pay fair market rents?

If one asks the simple question, "Were commercial businesses actually displaced by loft converters?," the simple answer is "yes." If landlords were willing to continue renting commercial spaces at prevailing rates, they would probably have retained manufacturers who wanted to stay in business. Landlords were unlikely to do this when larger profits could be made by renting to residential tenants, or by selling their buildings to cooperatives and developers.

Rapkin (1963) argued that the existing businesses in SoHo, most of which employed blue-collar workers, were a healthy part of the general economic structure of New York. Rapkin's study, however, was probably overly optimistic, primarily because he assumed that a good number of these firms would continue to operate at the margins of New York's economy. The decline that Rapkin reported in 1963 did not stop, however, but continued into the 1970s. Nonetheless, a number of firms that Rapkin studied remain in SoHo despite all the conversions that took place and the increasing demand for loft spaces for residential housing.

The issue, however, is not simply a question of profit: it is more complicated. The conversion of loft space to residential use does not always constitute displacement. One industrial or craft activity can replace another: urban areas can change in their economic function. For those who were concerned about actual displacement of manufacturing in New York, the question was whether or not commercial tenants were able to move to some other location in the city or had to close or move out altogether. For the city as an economic entity, it is one thing to have a business shift its location—the history of New York is replete with the redistribution of commercial and industrial activity. It is quite another to have the business depart from the city, with the resultant loss of jobs, revenues, and factories.

In the late 1970s, New York's economic planners and those who were responsible for encouraging business growth in the city were worried that unchecked displacement would result in serious consequences for New York's economy. The growing concern over the future led to an increased demand for control over loft conversions. The first step was more vigorous efforts to help existing firms find alternative spaces when these businesses were faced with displacement; the second, detailed in Chapter 6, was to demand new and more stringent zoning codes for Lower Manhattan. These actions helped slow residential loft conversion down in the late 1970s.

Turning now to the impact of developers on the loft conversion movement: there is good evidence that they significantly altered the process. "Around 1975, through the influence of the professional developers' housing criteria, lofts showed more conventional relations between space, time, and money. The legal clearance and bank financing that professional developers obtained paved the way to more extensive, as well as intensive, development of loft buildings" (Zukin, 1982:130). Developers began realizing the economic opportunities in converting entire buildings, and, unlike the initial pioneers and, later, more affluent middle-class loft converters, they were more interested in profits than in the values associated with art, neighborhood, community, and life-style. But they were quite ready to use these values in advertising their buildings and to capitalize on the myths associated with the new urban communities of SoHo, NoHo, and TriBeCa.

Professional developers depend upon bank financing, and banks are reluctant to finance activities that are as blatantly illegal as the conversion of loft buildings. Legal conversions, then, might reveal the extent of professional developers' activities. In Midtown South (the area below Grand Central Station and above Fourteenth Street), for example, one of the most active areas of loft conversion outside SoHo, NoHo, and TriBeCa, legal conversions were quite limited. By 1977, 320 buildings were being converted—310 illegally. As Zukin reports (1982:138–39), some developers were involved in these illegal conversions, but these were probably marginal actors in loft conversions in this area, accounting for only a few of the buildings being converted.

Even when they could get the needed zoning variances and carry out conversions legally, developers might be reluctant to continue converting older buildings indefinitely. There are market limits, and as more buildings are converted, profit margins shrink. When all things are considered, loft conversion and the recycling of older buildings have a somewhat limited market (Salins, 1979). Developers played an important, if limited, role in the loft conversion activity in Lower Manhattan in the late 1970s, but both legal and market restrictions kept the number of commercial spaces being converted by professional developers to a small proportion of the total.

Zukin's claim (1982:11; 135–40) that professional developers became the most important force in the loft conversion process does not have support in the information others have gathered (Ballinson, 1981; Simpson, 1982). That information does, however, indicate that developers probably did assist in the legalization of loft conversions. They also probably contributed to the pressure for zoning changes and other government responses. The aggregate data suggest that developers occupied only the tip—albeit a profitable pinnacle—of the loft conversion iceberg.

The growing strength of the market for residential lofts was reflected in the changing costs for development of loft spaces. There are no comprehensive data on the cost of loft spaces in New York City, and this is true whether one is looking at the price of a loft building, the rents charged, or the costs of conversion.[1] There are various sources, however, that will give a general idea about the economics of loft living; while these data are limited to SoHo, they can be taken as representative of the general patterns in loft rent and building prices, and are probably low for the entire Lower Manhattan area considering the data on assessed value given in Chapters 2 and 5.

In 1977, the *Village Voice* published an article on the changing costs of loft space in SoHo which reported that in the early days, pioneer artists "were paying $90 for 3,000 square feet of space. Granted it was splintered, arid space, but the landlords were grateful for any renters, and the streets had a dada elegance" (March 21, 1977:22). That rent comes to thirty-six cents per square foot per year. The *Economist* ("Artists Aloft," 1963) reported a rent of $35 per month for a loft floor. Even if the figures are biased toward the low end, they indicate how low rents were in the early days. Certainly rents were commonly under $200 for "large" loft space, and fell below $100 on occasion. The cheapest spaces were "only wall to wall floors," or what was called "raw space." There is some agreement among sources that loft spaces were renting for between $1.30 and $1.80 per square foot before 1970, and that by 1975 this had increased to about $1.80 to $2.75. Such a rate is well below the cost of a standard apartment in Manhattan, which in 1975 rented for an average of $6.00 per square foot (Zukin, 1982:143–48; Simpson, 1981:233–37). Rent for a loft floor that was not "finished" was about $225 in 1972, and had increased to about $500 by 1980. Ballinson cites another study by the *Village Voice* which reports that a 1,500-square-foot loft rented for about $175 in 1970, but had gone up to $875 by 1980 (1981:31).

Another measure of change in loft prices can be seen in the differences in the cost of the first artist cooperatives in 1967 and 1968 and the price of a co-op floor ten years later. The 1967–68 purchase prices ranged from $60,000 to $210,000 per building. By contrast, a co-op floor in 1976 was priced for raw space from $30,000 to $60,000, and for finished space from $80,000 to $130,000. In 1982, one building with few amenities was being turned into co-ops in which a "reasonable" price for half a floor was $86,000; and a half floor in another loft building was sold in the same year for $140,000, as contrasted to the original 1969 price for the entire floor of $10,000.

The initial converters of loft spaces had to invest a good deal of time and money to make those spaces habitable. As these conversions progressed, and as the amounts invested increased, those who left these spaces asked for and received "fixture fees," i.e., reimbursement for their investments in conversion. In 1972, fixture fees ranged between $2,500 and $5,000, depending upon the length of the lease obtainable. By 1980, this had increased to $8,000 to $15,000 (Simpson, 1981:234). While these figures are somewhat inexact, they indicate the significant degree of increase in loft prices. Rising costs for housing, even in the tight market of Manhattan, do result in limiting the possible pool of potential residents. There are probably limits on what the market will bear in terms of prices for loft spaces, and as the "bargains" in lofts became a memory, the demand also declined significantly.

The rise in the price of loft buildings and the increase in loft rents began in the late 1960s, and its impact was the source of worry for many who wanted to maintain SoHo's integrity as an artistic community. In 1970, *New York Magazine* published an article, "SoHo: Artists' Bohemia Imperiled," that voiced the concern that was to be reiterated during the subsequent decade: that the low rents that artists could afford would no longer be available as SoHo became more "respectable" and attractive. By 1977, the *Village Voice* claimed in an article, "SoHo Loft for Sale: Artists Need Not Apply":

As SoHo has grown in prestige, so have the fortunes made in quasi-legal speculation and transference of cooperative stock.

That many of the profiteers are artists, and they had no entre-
preneurial interests before SoHo was created, is one of the signal
ironies of life in this district. What was mandated by the best
minds in city government as a haven for beleaguered artists has
become a real-estate boondoggle, attracting what the critic Lucy
Lippard calls "a geography of boutiques, bars, and fancy food."
And artists who can't afford the price are moving out. (Goldstein, 3/21/77:72)

The artists had pioneered an urban area only to see the process of
succession produce a gentrified neighborhood of loft housing that
was now priced beyond their means. Nonetheless a larger number
of artists, particularly those who had joined a co-op, were able to
remain in SoHo, and there were still lofts that artists who arrived
in the late 1970s and early 1980s could afford.

The loft areas of Lower Manhattan have passed through a tumul-
tuous period of social change and have attained a new equilibrium.
There are now extended families in the area. Children have grown
up knowing no other life-style than loft living with parents who
work "at home" (for more details on family life in SoHo, see
Simpson, 1981: Chapter 10).

   As the neighborhood has stabilized, the open community of the
late 1960s and early 1970s has become a more "closed" community, in which formal relations prevail. There are strong social
networks that continue to defend the neighborhood; they are less
tenuous and experimental than they were just a few years ago.
While there are communal efforts like day care facilities for the
children, these areas still do not have their own schools or
churches, and the stores that have opened are more likely to serve
the affluent and the tourists than the average resident. For daily
shopping, and for school and church, SoHo residents must commute, if only a few blocks, into Little Italy, Chinatown, or Greenwich Village.

   Businesses that serve the neighborhood industrial firms are still
operating as they have for years. The Eagle Restaurant on the
corner of Broadway and Spring Street continues to do a large
carry-out trade, catering to the blue-collar and clerical workers

employed in the commercial and industrial enterprises along Broadway and its cross streets, as it did before there was a SoHo. But few tourists patronize it, since it is just a greasy spoon with no particular charm except for those of us who like hearty breakfasts and the ambience of a short-order restaurant with its casual banter between patrons and employees.

The daily rhythms of commerce go on, bringing in a labor force to work in the industrial and commercial lofts. The streets are still littered with industrial refuse, although dog droppings are more in evidence than was the case in 1968 when I first began my visits to SoHo. A number of lofts in which I have been a guest are still lacking certain amenities because the owners do not have sufficient funds to complete their conversions into "finished" spaces. "Next year" the bathroom will finally be done, and then some "new" furniture will be added to replace that scavenged from the streets and the relatives.

Some streets abound with expensive restaurants, smart shops, and chic bars, and are jammed with tourists a good deal of the time. For the most part, the local residents avoid these tourist haunts except when they entertain visitors from the suburbs and the hinterlands. Blue-collar workers, artists, and tourists share the same streets, but not the same social milieux.

Two recent surveys (1983) of the area indicate the degree to which an equilibrium has been achieved. One was conducted by the SoHo Alliance (SA), and the other by the Department of City Planning of the City of New York (DCP). There were some differences in their methodologies, and a slightly different emphasis in each: the SA surveyed only SoHo, and included commercial as well as residential tenants; the DCP studied both SoHo and NoHo, but did not survey commercial tenants.

The SoHo Alliance's purpose in conducting its survey was to obtain data that could be used in its ongoing efforts to maintain SoHo's cohesiveness as an artistic community. This organization, the direct descendant of the SoHo Artists Association, is concerned with the intrusions of developers and gaudy tourist attractions that might adversely affect the integrity of the community, and it worries that SoHo may become too gentrified. The Department of City Planning's survey was "intended to aid the on-going

■ Midday traffic on the corner of Spring and West Broadway. There is little in this picture to indicate that this is a fashionable residential neighborhood. (Photo courtesy of Melvin Reichler and Judith Reichler.)

assessment of the special needs and conditions of the City's loft areas" (*SoHo/NoHo: Occupancy Survey*, 1985: Preface). Both studies provide a measure of the area's equilibrium. The DCP's report is limited to a descriptive analysis; it does not offer any interpretation of the data. The SA report does, and its observations support to a large extent the conclusions reached in this study.

The DCP study estimates that there are 8,700 people living in 3,900 households in SoHo/NoHo (3,700 in lofts and 200 in apartments). The SA study makes no estimate of the population size of SoHo: its data suggest that there are about 3,000 residential lofts there. Both studies agree that the bulk of the population growth has occurred in the last ten years.

These data are sufficiently comparable to provide an accurate profile of this population today. About half of the householders own their own loft spaces in cooperative buildings. The SA survey found that 67 percent of the households were childless, and the DCP estimated that about 17 percent of the population was under eighteen years of age. A quarter of all households have only one member.

The average length of residence in the SoHo Alliance sample was 7.25 years, although 30 percent had lived in their lofts for more than ten years. The DCP survey found that 48 percent of the households had been there for six or more years, and of these half had been residents for ten or more years. The SA survey also indicated an important difference between loft owners and renters: "Loft cooperators tend not only to occupy spaces larger than renters, but also to have been in residence longer. The average cooperative loft space is 2,580 square feet . . . as opposed to the tenant average of 1,605, and the average co-opper has been in place 8.1 years as compared with the rental average of 6.5 years . . ." (*SoHo Survey*, 1983: Section 2.4). These data suggest that the cooperative residents are the most stable part of the population; given the fact of ownership, they will probably remain in SoHo longer than renters, maintaining the stability of SoHo's population.

I have argued in Chapter 6 that the zoning ordinances of 1981, together with increased attention to the provisions of the early zoning codes, have contributed to the stability of these areas (for example, by maintaining a balance between residential and commercial use of loft buildings). Stability does not mean that the loft area's population may not continue to grow; and there will be changes in these areas, but these will be influenced by the provisions of the 1981 zoning ordinances. The point is that SoHo and other loft areas have settled down considerably: routine rather than confusion and uncertainty is common. Future developments can be more predictable than was possible in the past, because the city's agencies have again asserted their authority over the land use patterns of the loft areas. Their actions will be monitored and influenced by the organizations that have played such an important role in establishing the current equilibrium in these areas.

The SoHo Alliance study validates other major conclusions of my analysis regarding the degree to which a new equilibrium has been established. "A great many artists remain in SoHo, they have lived there for quite some time, and their rents are *not* the astronomical figures often quoted in newspaper ads" (about 46 percent of the sample households paid less than $600.00 per month for their lofts). The SA survey "also suggests that manufacturing is not dead in SoHo, and that, surprisingly, both business people and residents are in close agreement on issues that affect the SoHo community" (*SoHo Survey*, 1983: Section 2:1). For example, 78 percent of the resident respondents opposed new residential construction, as did 68 percent of the commercial respondents; 86 and 89 percent respectively opposed discos, and 90 percent of the residents opposed high-rises, while 81 percent of the commercial tenants shared that opinion. Such consensus predicts that SoHo can be mobilized to challenge any fundamental alterations of the land use patterns in the area in the immediate future.

The SoHo Alliance survey summed up its findings by stating that "there is a very stable residential component within SoHo. . . . This neighborhood is not the 'revolving door' many people claim it to be" (*SoHo Survey*, 1983: Section 2:1). About 65 percent of the households contain a person certified (or eligible to be certified) as an artist according to the criteria used by the Artist Certification Committee of the Department of Cultural Affairs. Even among those who have lived there for three years or less, the number who gave "artist" as their occupation was exactly half. These data support the conclusion that SoHo is still a place where working artists seek to establish themselves.

As the SA study notes, one good reason for SoHo's continued attraction for artists can be summed up in a "single word: 'supply.' Available within a few blocks of any SoHo loft are all the tools and materials the artist could need: a choice of lumber yards, artist supply and paint stores, plastics and glass companies, electrical and plumbing places, electronic outlets, hardware stores, machine tool rental and sales centers, textile and paper companies, as well as the myriad of hard-to-define items available along Canal Street. The availability of these artist-related materials (as well as the 'found-in-the-street' leftovers of local business) continues to be a magnet to the artist moving in" (*SoHo Survey*, 1983: Section 2:6). The Department of City Planning's survey reports that 82 percent of the artists purchase their materials in SoHo/NoHo proper (*SoHo/NoHo: Occupancy Survey*, 1985:46).

"The SoHo Alliance concludes from the survey that artists still abound in SoHo, that residents and business exist side-by-side, and residential communities within SoHo support our battle to prevent nonconforming uses from taking over our neighborhood" (*SoHo Survey*, 1983: Section 2:7). As one of the leading organizations defending SoHo from possible future transformations, the Alliance is guardedly optimistic about its ability to influence the future land use patterns there. As a veteran of a number of struggles to regulate SoHo's social and economic development, it has achieved a measure of success in helping the loft areas of Lower Manhattan attain their current equilibrium.

Some Patterns in the Postindustrial City

The success of SoHo artists, as well as others, in developing and defending a new urban community, and the actions taken by residents in a number of other cities to renovate and restore old neighborhoods or recycle industrial buildings to residential use, suggest that the decline of some older cities may be reversed— even if only in certain areas. All older cities may not be attractive to a large number of middle-class households, and perhaps only a few areas within them can be maintained as middle-class neighborhoods. So much attention has been given to urban gentrification and the yuppies, however, that we have overlooked the solid working-class neighborhoods in these cities. Their presence and vitality demonstrate that the "good life" the city offers is not reserved for the elite and special segments of the middle class. Instead, it can be argued that working-class neighborhoods are part of the future of older cities. The problems posed by the urban poor, racially and ethnically disadvantaged, and neglected elderly remain grave. Obviously, if these problems are going to be solved, there will have to be substantial changes in social policies at the federal, state, and local levels.

A number of older manufacturing cities can still attract industry; they have well-developed infrastructures (some needing extensive repairs); cadres of skilled and unskilled workers; favorable market locations; and political leaders actively engaged in retaining and recruiting businesses of all kinds. A large number of urban problems might be lessened if the economies of these cities were to become stronger, and political reputations can be made by those who can successfully restore them to health.[2] There is guarded optimism about New York's future as a manufacturing center (Hughes and Sternlieb, 1978; Rapkin, 1963), and recent evidence, in fact, points to a strong recovery in manufacturing in many northeastern cities (Lueck, 1985).

One cannot reasonably conclude for these cities, as Smith did for New York, that "all that is left . . . is what economist Michael Rubin calls the 'knowledge shell'—a cadre of management and clerical stalls linked to support groups of lawyers, accountants, and media specialists who merchandise the status jeans with high voltage advertising" (1981:27). New York and other older cities appear to have more resiliency than they have been credited with. Their adaptations may take some unanticipated directions, like that of the loft conversion movement in Lower Manhattan. The study of such unanticipated changes gives us a firmer basis for making more accurate predictions about the future direction of our cities, and increases our ability to design effective policies to assist their transformation into economically successful communities.

Another major reason why older cities need not be seen as suffering from terminal illness is the strong allure they continue to have for many of us. They offer what cities have offered for centuries: a vitality and life-style that can provide a wide range of cultural and social options, encouraging personal freedom and individual choice. Before we relegate our cities to the status of anachronisms, we should consider their continued power to attract and stimulate many members of contemporary society.

Many of our cities have squares, plazas, and boulevards that were created to promote large-scale celebrations; their monumental architecture and historically significant buildings are focal points for society's ceremonies. We turn to our cities when we wish to stage nationally important events: the Olympics, the World Fairs, the parades for returning veterans and hostages. Demonstrations for peace, civil rights, or national unity take on an added significance when their backdrops are symbolically significant urban spaces, rich with history and social meaning.

Our cities can provide the stages for such events because, in addition to their imposing locales, they have the political organization needed to mount, support, and control such celebrations. These political and economic resources are not their only reasons for sponsoring them, however: the self-image these cities wish to project and maintain make them eager candidates for the privilege of holding these events (Suttles, 1984), even when the expenditures seem to exceed the returns. The investment in the city's image and future is seen as justifying any losses incurred.

Many older cities now contain permanent "fairs" located in recently revived harbor areas and historical districts, like Baltimore's Inner Harbor, New York's South Street Seaport, and Boston's Faneuil Hall. Part of their attraction is their location within a functioning urban context. They blend into the city's landscape and become part of its urban texture. They generate an urban vitality that spreads beyond their immediate location, calling attention to the other parts of the city that offer additional opportunities for urban adventure.

Neighborhoods that celebrate local culture still flourish in our cities; they not only provide entertainment, but are an integral part of the communities in which they occur. Chinese New Year in the

Chinatowns, church festivals in the Little Italies, the ethnic fetes of Greeks, Swedes, Irish, and Germans not only reinforce the integration of these communities, but are also part of our shared culture. New areas like SoHo also provide festivals that celebrate the local community (Glueck, 1976; MacBean, 1980).

But the "city as festival" exists not only in large-scale celebrations in the public plazas, "fairs" in the new entertainment districts, or fetes in local community neighborhoods; nor does it reside solely in the excitement of panoramic views from the Empire State Building, the Sears Tower, or the Gateway Arch in St. Louis. The celebration of urban life is also found in the enjoyment of urban facilities that some daily users take for granted—the Staten Island Ferry, the cable cars of San Francisco, the walkway over the Brooklyn Bridge, the Public Garden in Boston, the Mall in Washington, D.C., the Pike Street Market in Seattle, and the boat houses along the Schuylkill River in Philadelphia. It is broadcast in city magazines that sing their praises, chronicle their foibles, and cater to the tastes of urban dwellers.

We are, for better or worse, an urban society. The concept of city as festival has become increasingly attractive, primarily because urban experience is impossible outside these older central cities. Suburban communities simply do not have the architecture, the history, or the political organization to mount urban celebrations. Shopping malls can be "monumental," but they have no sense of place. They are so artificial that there is little opportunity for the chance discoveries that are part of urban life. No one can be as sophisticated about "knowing" a mall as one can be about "knowing" a city and the excitement that its various neighborhoods, communities, and districts offer.

Unfortunately, many of the new urban cores that have been built to "save" the cities are almost equally devoid of this aura of celebration and adventure. The overwhelming presence of most newly constructed office buildings dwarfs the human scale of social activities. It is difficult to find a place to sit or lean to which a tariff is not attached. One can hardly be casual in such surroundings, and the entertainment provided is restricted to the affluent and expense account elite. When the offices close and the traffic departs, there is little left for those who wish to socialize informally.

The city as festival comes into being in its most genuine forms where the opportunity to participate in the most positive aspects of the urban experience exists. It is in the streets, shops, stores, and restaurants that offer us the chance to demonstrate our abilities to be sophisticated participants in the modern urban world. The population is a mixture of races, ethnic groups, and classes. The city as festival is one idealized image of American society come to life—open, tolerant, a sort of global village.

Whatever the root causes of our segregated society, many of us find it constricting. We would like to live in a more open society, one in which we can be active participants, expressing ourselves more fully. The city as festival provides an opportunity to participate in urban culture, a culture that is richly embedded in the images of our cities (Suttles, 1984). It represents a chance to escape from the narrow aspects of our lives. It is little wonder that our cities are attracting an increasing number of visitors seeking such experiences, and that many are finding these older cities appealing places to live.

The mass media have picked up on these themes. Their focus is not on the patios of suburbia, on which a permanent pall of ennui has descended. The homogenized suburban society has little appeal or zest. The growth of the entertainment sector in our society reflects this need for excitement. Often is it packaged into theme parks and is presented as authentic while it is nothing more than kitsch. The revitalized areas of our cities, and those that have sustained their essence during the period of urban decline are much more genuine. A place like SoHo epitomizes what cities are all about: people really work there; the life of the community and the lives of the people flow together; and those who live, work, and visit there are active participants in its social life.

There are those who argue that the central city's advantageous sites should be given over to more office buildings, to luxury housing for the corporate and entertainment elites, to large transportation exchanges or sophisticated hospitals and bio-tech, to wholesale trade and yet larger trade shows, to vast containerized port facilities, to more massive government buildings—indeed to anything other than areas for urban communal experience. Despite the economic logic of these opinions, the evidence indicates that the city can and does offer an opportunity for personal and social experiences that cannot be duplicated outside it. The city's ecosystem is not simply a producing and consuming economy driven by market forces: it is a "natural" social system that blends economic, political, and cultural components into a vibrant whole.

Toward Refining Ecological Theory

The central thesis of this study is that human ecology continues to offer a distinctive and effective perspective from which to identify, interpret, predict, and suggest plans to control urban social change. In establishing ecology's comprehensive effectiveness for studying urban social systems, an effort has been made to illustrate the broad areas that are within the theory's analytic range: economic forces and cultural patterns, the effects of historical social processes, and the conscious actions of social actors.

Ecological theory has often been presented and interpreted in ways that have ignored, neglected, or obscured the active and effective role of individuals and groups in the process of change or movement toward equilibrium. Critics of ecological theory have attacked its usefulness as an analytic scheme for understanding and explaining social systems on the basis that the theory has failed to consider the significant effects of conscious social action by individuals, groups, and governments on the process of adaptation to the environment, or on changing the environment itself (Alihan, 1938; Firey, 1947; Willhelm, 1962; Zeitz, 1979). This study, like others (Hawley, 1963; Duncan, 1961; Berry and Kasarda, 1977; Catton, 1980), demonstrates clearly that ecological theory can readily handle such variables as conscious social action; and, indeed, that it must if comprehensive explanations of current social systems are to be made, and if the call from some ecologists for conscious actions to change social policies having a detrimental impact on our environment (and, in the long run, our chances for survival on this planet) is to be effectively heeded (Bennett, 1976; Berry and Kasarda, 1977; Catton, 1980; Campbell, 1983).

This study would have been incomplete without its consideration of the role of organized groups and actors that influenced the processes analyzed and the patterns identified and explained. It did not depend solely upon outmoded concepts like "pure markets," "natural competition," and "subsocial" levels to analyze the ecology of Lower Manhattan, but recognized, as have most contemporary ecological theorists, that conscious and deliberate actions by individuals and groups are part of the analytic framework of ecology. It follows the lead of Berry and Kasarda in recognizing that our increased knowledge about how social systems work can result in our ability to use the discipline of ecology to shape the ecosystems of the future (1977:429).[3]

I believe that ecology's domain should be consciously expanded to include unique individual examples of social change as well as the more comparative studies that have marked human ecology's important contribution to sociology; that the traditional coarse-grained model of ecology should be refined to allow for a fine-grained analysis of processes such as the ones examined in this study. Such a refinement cannot help but enhance ecology's capacity to provide a comprehensive understanding of such phenomena.

Ecological theory already offers some predictive insights as to when and how human actions will act to influence the social system (Duncan, 1961; Hawley, 1950:210–11; Hawley, 1963; Catton, 1980) as well as the general ecosystem (Bennett, 1976; Catton, 1980; Campbell, 1983). The theory does not stipulate that the actors will be successful, nor that the objectives they consciously pursue will be realized. But that they can have an effect has been demonstrated in this research, and the data indicate that their actions can contribute significantly to the establishment of a certain equilibrium, as ecological theory predicts. Whatever stability the artistic community of SoHo now enjoys has been, in large part, the result of the actions of groups and individuals in shaping the existing land use patterns and the development of the flourishing community now found there.

The decline in New York's manufacturing businesses was part of a complex ecological process that has been documented. The loss of manufacturing in Lower Manhattan opened loft spaces to a new population—pioneer artists. The initial invasion of artists did not take place according to any preconceived plan to alter land use patterns. The changes the artists initiated, however, led to a number of subsequent changes that might more appropriately be called stages. Each subsequent stage involved more conscious action on the part of those concerned with and affected by these changes. As it developed its own patterns and organization, the local culture began to exert a more pervasive influence on the process. The unanticipated and unplanned process of loft conversion became more predictable as the stages progressed and the actors most affected began to institutionalize and stabilize the emerging land use patterns. Tenant organizations, city agencies, developers, and the mass media all participated in shaping the outcome of the loft conversion process. A good deal of what began as a seemingly serendipitous phenomenon became planned and coordinated.

Some of the underlying forces that supported and sustained ecological succession in Lower Manhattan were beyond the control of the city government, the organized groups, and the individual actors. Others were not. Some of the limits of control were embedded in the city's political structure; others were imposed by New York's economic organization; still others were the result of exogenous and endogenous forces which could not even accurately be perceived, let alone controlled. Even with these limits, there was room to maneuver and to take conscious actions that clearly led to more stable conditions in what had been an extremely chaotic situation.

The new land use patterns in Lower Manhattan were created through the processes of invasion, succession, and adaptation. There is now a new equilibrium in this area that has reached its most complete expression in a new urban community, SoHo. The exogenous and endogenous variables that produced the current social order there interacted reciprocally and cumulatively, reenforcing the direction of change and, in the final analysis, Lower Manhattan's stability. Neither set of variables appears to have been more influential in producing this outcome, but both are critical to explaining the ecological processes that shaped the loft areas.

What did happen with loft conversions in Lower Manhattan was clearly novel: a human ecology, such as that applied here, can provide an explanatory framework that is not only retrospectively descriptive, but has the potential for more accurate prediction. And our ability to predict has more than just an academic value. It can be used to help us develop and execute policies that will increase our chances to adapt constructively to an ever changing and challenging environment.

Notes

Chapter 1. Human Ecology

1   A detailed presentation of those findings can be found in Laska and Spain (1980) and in *Urban Affairs Quarterly* (June 1980).

2   There has been no attempt to keep the elements of these various disciplines distinct in this presentation. There have also been a number of other studies using different orientations that have covered the issue being analyzed. See for example, Ballinson (1981), Ford (1978), Simpson (1981), and Zukin (1982).

3   The general symbolic importance of space has been the subject of an increasing literature that questions the influence of an unfettered market. Firey's work (1947) demonstrated the validity of a more refined interpretation and claimed that ecology could not handle the alternative explanations. Hawley, however, in his review (1947) of Firey's monograph, did not view the findings as inconsistent with his general theoretical orientation that location and value are positively correlated.

4   For a more complete discussion of these and related issues, see Alonso (1970), Bourne (1969), Brigham (1965), R. J. Johnston (1971), and Muth (1969).

5   This process may vary depending upon the society studied, but these cultural differences have been incorporated into the general theoretical model (Theodorson, 1982:353–464).

Chapter 2. Invasion-Succession in SoHo

1   The way in which SoHo was named remains something of a mystery. There are four different explanations in the literature, one in Stratton (1977:31) and three in Simpson (1980:1, 150, 163).

143

2 For richer details of the early history of SoHo and other parts of Lower Manhattan, see Koch (1976), Simpson, (1981: especially pp. 111–18), and Toll (1969: especially pp. 35–116).

3 An interesting sidelight on this movement was provided by the actions taken by the Fifth Avenue merchants to stop the incursions of loft manufacturing near their retail outlets by lobbying successfully for the first zoning regulations in the United States. The shift uptown of loft buildings is graphically described in Toll's discussion, "Up the Avenue" (1969:74–116).

4 This information comes from a personal interview with Macuinas. For a more complete account of Macuinas, see Simpson (1981:155–66) and Goldberg (1977). Other artists had moved into loft buildings around Coentiss Slip in Lower Manhattan in the middle 1950s (Stratton, 1977:24; Tompkins, 1980). Art production in lofts is well documented in Eckhardt and Düttman (1976).

Chapter 3. The Social Environment of SoHo's Development

1 The development of Abstract Expressionism fits the general pattern that Becker (1982) has identified in his analysis of "art worlds." In particular, see his Chapter 1, "Art Worlds and Collective Activity," and Chapter 10, "Changes in Art Worlds."

2 The recycling of commercial and industrial spaces to help alleviate some of the inner city problems of decay and decline was not unique to New York. Studies of reusing of old buildings have been reported in Roddewig (1981), Bunnell (1977), and Economic Benefits of Preserving Old Buildings (1976).

Chapter 4. Social Dynamics in SoHo

1 The SAA represents the human ecological concept of a "categoric group," "an association of functionally homogeneous individuals" or groups (Hawley, 1950:210). It is "characteristically reactive, and its function is to conserve or protect what is necessary to the welfare of its members" (Hawley, 1950:211). The details and dynamics of this organization are not included here, but have been well presented in Simpson (1981).

2 A comprehensive description of the community press can be found in Janowitz. In particular, Janowitz argues that in large cities, the "development of . . . satellite business districts reflected changes in the population along community lines and created an audience that could be addressed in

terms of local geographical identification" (1952:22). Such was the case with SoHo, with its growing number of galleries, restaurants, and shops.

3   Caroline F. Ware expresses this sentiment in her analysis of Greenwich Village in the 1920s. "In the post-War years, the old group of artists gradually broke up and drifted away, leaving behind them the echo of their renown and the oft-repeated question, 'Is the Village still the literary capital of America? What has become of those who give it its fame? Has the artist colony of the village been supplied with new blood as the years have gone by?' " (1965:241).

Chapter 5. The Expansion of the Loft Conversion Movement

1   The richness and variety can be appreciated by reviewing such volumes as Paul Goldberger (1979) and Lehnartz and Talbot (1978).

2   The pattern of loft conversions below Fifty-ninth Street excluding SoHo. As was the case for SoHo, the data presented represent only loft buildings as defined by the Real Property Assessment Department.

Chapter 6. The Political Response to Loft Conversions in Lower Manhattan

1   I worked as a volunteer consultant on that research in 1980.

2   The J-51 program was one of those measures cities had adopted to stem the process of urban decay by offering economic incentives to land developers to provide renewed housing to the middle classes. For more detailed information on the J-51 program, see Goldin (1980); Ford (1978), especially Chapter 5, "The Fiscal Impact of the J-51 Program to Encourage Residential Conversions"; and New York State Office of Development Planning (1980).

Chapter 7. Conclusion and Implications

1   Caroline F. Ware was confronted with the same problem in her study of Greenwich Village in the 1920s. "An exact index of the rent increases which encouraged and reflected the successive stages of reconstruction could not be compiled because the complete lack of standardization in remodeled buildings made comparisons virtually impossible. Informal evidence, however, mounts up to indicate the reality of rent increases in the remodeled houses and apartments" (1965:20).

2   Harvey Molotch has provided us with some useful insights on how

political and economic elites might respond to these changing conditions. While his persuasive arguments about the "city as a growth machine" are well founded as an interpretation of early patterns, I also concur with him that it now becomes possible "to utilize national institutions to effect other policies, which both solidify the death of the growth machine at the local level and create national priorities consistent with the new opportunities for civic life" (Molotch, 1976:329). It should be noted that Molotch is not writing from a human ecological perspective.

3 Bennett has also argued for this recognition in his argument for a more comprehensive definition of human ecology that would include "a pattern of purposive behavior involving a matching of resources with objectives, and a capacity to think about this process objectively without actually going through the physical steps. This form of behavior also contains the capacity of becoming aware of the disturbances created by humans in the milieu, and how these might be avoided if there is evidence of danger" (1976:35–36).

Bibliography

Action Plan: Report of Mayor's Task Force on Loft Conversions. 1978.

Aldrich, Howard. "Ecological Succession in Racially Changing Neighborhoods: A Review of the Literature." *Urban Affairs Quarterly* 10, no. 3 (March 1975): 327–48.

Aldrich, Howard, and Albert J. Reiss, Jr. "Continuities in the Study of Ecological Succession: Changes in the Race Composition and Their Neighborhood Business." *American Journal of Sociology* 81, no. 4 (January 1976): 846–66.

Alihan, Milla A. *Social Ecology.* New York: Columbia University Press, 1938.

Alonso, William. *Location and Land Use: Toward a General Theory of Land Rent.* Cambridge: Harvard University Press, 1970.

"Artists Aloft." *The Economist,* April 6, 1963:43.

Ballinson, James P. *Regulating Loft Conversions in New York City: Better Late Than Never.* Senior thesis, Princeton University, 1981.

Becker, Howard S. *Art Worlds.* Berkeley: University of California Press, 1982.

Bennett, John W. *The Ecological Transition: Cultural Anthropology and Human Adaptation.* New York: Pergamon Press, 1976.

Bernard, Jessie. *The Sociology of Community.* Glenview, Ill.: Scott, Foresman and Company, 1973.

Berry, Brian J. L., and John D. Kasarda. *Contemporary Urban Ecology.* New York: Macmillan Publishing Co., 1977.

Bourne, L. S. "Location Factors in the Redevelopment Process: A Model of Residential Change." *Land Economics* 65, no. 2 (May 1969): 183–93.

Brigham, Eugene F. "The Determination of Residential Land Values." *Land Economics* 41, no. 4 (November 1965): 325–34.

Bunnell, Gene. *Built to Last: A Handbook on Recycling Old Buildings.* Washington, D.C.: The Preservation Press, 1977.

Burgess, Ernest W. "The Growth of the City: An Introduction to a Research Project." In Robert E. Park, Ernest W. Burgess, and R. D. McKenzie, eds., *The City* (Chicago: University of Chicago Press, 1925).

Byrd, C. L. *SoHo.* New York: Doubleday, 1981.

Campbell, Bernard. *Human Ecology: The Story of Our Place in Nature From Prehistory to the Present.* London: Heinemann Educational Books, 1983.

Catton, William R., Jr. *Overshoot: The Ecological Basis of Revolutionary Change.* Urbana: University of Illinois Press, 1980.

Clay, Philip L. *Neighborhood Renewal: Middle-Class Resettlement and Incumbent Upgrading in American Neighborhoods.* Lexington, Mass.: Lexington Books, 1979.

Cressey, Paul F. "Population Succession in Chicago: 1898–1930." *American Journal of Sociology* 44 (July 1938): 59–69.

Davis, Douglas. *Art and the Future: A History/Prophecy of the Collaboration Between Science, Technology and Art.* New York: Praeger Publishers, 1973.

———. "SoHo du mal: Film, Video, Culture, Politics." In Eckhardt and Düttman (1976).

Duncan, Otis Dudley. "From Social System to Ecosystem." *Sociological Inquiry* 31, no. 2 (Spring 1961): 140–49.

Duncan, Otis Dudley, and Beverly Duncan. *The Negro Population of Chicago: A Study of Residential Succession.* Chicago: University of Chicago Press, 1957.

Eckhardt, Ulrich, and Werner Düttman, eds. *New York—Downtown Manhattan: SoHo.* Berlin: Akademie der Künste-Berliner Festwochen, 1976.

Economic Benefits of Preserving Old Buildings. Proceedings of a conference held in Seattle, July 31–August 2, 1975. Washington, D.C.: The Preservation Press, 1976.

Firey, Walter. *Land Use in Central Boston.* Cambridge: Harvard University Press, 1947.

Fischer, Claude S. *The Urban Experience.* New York: Harcourt Brace Jovanovich, 1976.

Fischler, Stan. *Uptown, Downtown: A Trip Through Time on New York's Subways.* New York: Hawthorn Books, 1976.

Fitcher, R. Young. *Professionals and City Neighborhoods.* Boston: Parkman Center for Urban Affairs, 1977.

Ford, Kristina. *Housing Policy & the Urban Middle Class.* New Brunswick, N.J.: Center for Urban Policy Research, 1978.

Frank, Peter. "New York Fluxus." In Eckhardt and Düttman (1976).

Freiberg, Peter. "How Now, NoHo—New Zoning for Lofty Living?" *New York Post,* June 18, 1975.

Freundenburg, William R. "Succession and Success: A New Look at an Old Concept." *Sociological Spectrum* 5 (1985): 269–89.

Gale, Dennis E. "The Back-to-the-City Movement Revisited: A Recent Survey of Homebuyers in the Capitol Hill Neighborhood of Washington, D.C." Washington, D.C.: George Washington University, Department of Urban and Regional Planning, 1977.

Gamson, William A. *Power and Discontent.* Homewood, Ill.: The Dorsey Press, 1968.

Gardner, Paul. "SoHo: Brave New Bohemia." *Art News* 73, no. 4 (April 1974): 56–57.

Gayle, Margot, and Edward Gillon, Jr. *Cast-Iron Architecture in New York.* New York: Dover Publications, 1974.

Glueck, Grace. "A Celebration in SoHo." *New York Times,* June 11, 1976: C–1, 15.

Goldberger, Paul. *The City Observed: New York.* New York: Vintage Books, 1979.

Goldin, Harrison J. "J–51 Tax Abatement and Tax Exemption Housing Benefits: Emerging Policy Issues, With a Focus on Conversions." New York City: Office of the Comptroller, October 20, 1980.

Goldstein, Richard. "SoHo Loft for Sale: Artists Need Not Apply." *Village Voice,* March 21, 1977: 22–26.

Grier, George, and Eunice Grier. "Urban Displacement: A Reconnaissance." In Laska and Spain (1980).

Griffin, Donald W., and Richard E. Preston. "A Restatement of the 'Transition Zone' Concept." *Annals of the Association of American Geographers* 56, nos. 2–4 (1966): 339–50.

Guilbaut, Serge. *How New York Stole the Idea of Modern Art: Abstract Expressionism, Freedom, and the Cold War.* Chicago: University of Chicago Press, 1983.

Hamnett, Christopher, and Peter R. Williams. "Social Change in London: A Study of Gentrification." *Urban Affairs Quarterly* 15, no. 6 (June 1980): 469–87.

Harris, C. D., and E. L. Ullman. "The Nature of Cities." *Annals of the American Academy of Political and Social Sciences* 242 (1945): 7–17.

Hawley, Amos H. "Community Power and Urban Renewal Success." *American Journal of Sociology* 48, no. 4 (January 1963): 422–31.

———. "Ecology and Human Ecology." *Social Forces* 23 (May 1944): 398–405.

———. *Human Ecology: A Theory of Community Structure.* New York: Ronald Press, 1950.

———. "Human Ecology." In *International Encyclopedia of the Social Sciences,* vol. 4. New York: Macmillan Company and Free Press, 1968: 328–37.

———. *Urban Society: An Ecological Approach.* New York: Ronald Press, 1971.

———. "Walter Firey's *Land Use in Central Boston.*" Review in *American Sociological Review* 12 (1947): 358–60.

Hellman, Peter. "Loft Living: Can You Make It on the Urban Frontier?" *Apartment Life,* April 1977: 62–67.

Hollingshead, A. B. "A Re-examination of Ecological Theory." *Sociology and Social Research* 31 (January-February 1947): 194–204.

Hoover, Edgar M., and Raymond Vernon. *Anatomy of a Metropolis.* New York: Anchor Books, 1962.

Hornick, Sandy. "New York Plays Robin Hood in Loft Industries." *Planning* 48, no. 10 (November 1982): 18–21.

Houstoun, Lawrence O., Jr., and Feather O'Connor. "Neighborhood Change, Displacement and City Policy." In Laska and Spain (1980).

Hoyt, Homer. *The Structure and Growth of Residential Neighborhoods in American Cities.* Washington, D.C.: Federal Housing Administration, 1939.

Hudson, James R. "Changing Land-Use Patterns in SoHo: Residential Invasion of an Industrial Area." In Theodorson (1982).

———. "Ecological Theory and Inner City Revitalization." Paper presented at the Eastern Sociological Society Meetings, March 1979.

———. "Pioneer Artists and Middle-Class Settlers: Life-Style Variables and Neighborhood Succession." Paper presented at the Annual Meetings of the Midwest Sociological Society, Chicago, 1984.

Hughes, James W., and George Sternlieb. *Jobs & People: New York City 1985.* New Brunswick, N.J.: Center for Urban Policy Research, 1978.

Hunter, Albert. *Symbolic Communities: The Persistence and Change of Chicago's Neighborhoods.* Chicago: University of Chicago Press, 1974.

Hurd, Richard M. *Principles of City Land Values.* New York: Arno Press, 1970. (Originally published in 1903.)

Jacobs, Jane. *The Death and Life of Great American Cities.* New York: Vintage Books, 1961.

James, F. J. *Back to the City: An Appraisal of Housing Reinvestment and*

Population Change in Urban America. Washington, D.C.: The Urban
Institute, 1977.

Janowitz, Morris. *The Community Press in an Urban Setting.* Chicago:
University of Chicago Press, 1952.

———. "The Journalistic Profession and the Mass Media." In Joseph Ben
David and Terry Nichols Clark, eds., *Culture and Its Creators: Essays
in Honor of Edward Shils.* Chicago: University of Chicago Press,
1977.

———. *The Last Half-Century: Social Change and Politics in America.*
Chicago: University of Chicago Press, 1978.

Johnston, Laurie. "Tribeca Follows SoHo Footsteps, Gingerly." *New York
Times,* August 25, 1977: B–1.

Johnston, R. J. *Urban Residential Patterns: An Introductory Review.*
New York: Praeger Publishers, 1971.

Keller, Suzanne. *The Urban Neighborhood: A Sociological Perspective.*
New York: Random House, 1968.

Koch, Stephen. "Reflections on SoHo." In Eckhardt and Düttman (1976).

Kron, Joan. "Loft Living." *New York Magazine,* May 1974: 54.

Landmarks Preservation Commission. "SoHo—Cast Iron Historic Designation Report." New York, 1973.

Laska, Shirley Bradway, and Daphne Spain, eds. *Back to the City: Issues in
Neighborhood Renovation.* New York: Pergamon Press, 1980.

Lehnartz, Klaus, and Allan R. Talbot. *New York in the Sixties.* New York:
Dover Publications, 1978.

Lipton, S. Gregory. "Evidence of Central City Revival." *Journal of the
American Institute of Planners* 43 (April 1977): 136–47.

"Living Big in a Loft." *Life* 68, no. 11 (March 1970): 61–65.

Lofts: Balancing the Equities. New York City: Department of City Planning, 1981.

Lofts: Balancing the Equities. New York: The New York Department of
City Planning, 1981.

London, Bruce. "Gentrification as Urban Reinvasion: Some Preliminary
Definitional and Theoretical Considerations." In Laska and Spain
(1980).

Lueck, Thomas J. "Signs of Economic Revival Abound in Northeast." *New
York Times,* June 23, 1985: 1, 36.

Lyon, Danny. *The Destruction of Lower Manhattan.* New York: The
Macmillan Company, 1969.

MacBean, J. P. "SoHo." *Horizon* (October 1980): 54–62.

McKenzie, Roderick D. "The Ecological Approach to the Study of the Human Community." In Amos H. Hawley, ed., *Roderick D. McKenzie*

on Human Ecology (Chicago: University of Chicago Press, 1968):
33–48. First published in 1924.

———. "The Scope of Human Ecology." In Amos H. Hawley, ed., *Roderick
D. McKenzie on Human Ecology* (Chicago: University of Chicago
Press, 1968): 19–32. First published in 1926.

Manhattan Loft Rezoning Proposal. New York City: Department of City
Planning, March 1980. Prepared by Sandy Hornick and Suzanne
O'Keefe.

Merton, Robert K. "The Unanticipated Consequences of Purposive Social
Action." *American Sociological Review* 1, no. 6 (December 1936):
894–904.

Millstein, Gilbert. "Portrait of the Loft Generation." *New York Times
Magazine,* January 7, 1962: 24.

Molotch, Harvey Luskin. *Managed Integration: Dilemmas of Doing Good
in the City.* Berkeley: University of California Press, 1972.

———. "The City as a Growth Machine." *American Journal of Sociology*
82, no. 2 (September 1976): 309–32.

Muth, Richard F. *Cities and Housing: The Spatial Pattern of Urban Residential Land Use.* Chicago: University of Chicago Press, 1969.

Netzer, Dick. "The Arts: New York's Best Export Industry." *New York
Affairs* 5, no. 2 (1978): 50–61.

New York City. City Planning Commission. *Plan for New York City.*
1969.

New York State Office of Development Planning. *An Impact Review of
New York City's J–51 Program.* 1980.

Pantos, R. Andrew. "J–51 Conversions of Commercial and Industrial
Buildings in Manhattan: Effects on Displaced Businesses, and City/
State Payroll/Sales Tax Revenues." August 1980.

Park, Robert E. "Succession, An Ecological Concept." *American Sociological Review* 1, no. 2 (April 1936): 171–79.

"Population Study of Loft Tenants Occupying Manufacturing Space for
Residential Purposes." Association of Commercial Property Owners.
June 2, 1981.

President's Commission for a National Agenda in the Eighties. *Urban
America in the Eighties: Perspectives and Prospects.* Report of
the Panel on Policies and Prospects for Metropolitan and Non-
Metropolitan America. Washington, D.C.: U.S. Government Printing
Office, 1980.

Rapkin, Chester. *The South Houston Industrial Area.* New York City:
City Planning Commission, Department of City Planning, 1963.

Ratcliff, Carter. "SoHo: Disneyland of the Aesthete?" *New York Affairs* 4, no. 4 (1978): 64–72.

Residential Re-Use of Non Residential Buildings in Manhattan. New York City: Department of City Planning, 1977.

"Residential Status of Illegal Loft Conversions." New York City: Department of Housing Preservation & Development, September 1980.

Roddewig, J. *Loft Conversions: Planning Issues, Problems, and Prospects.* Chicago: American Planning Association, 1981.

Rogers, David. *Can Business Save the Cities?: The Case of New York.* New York: The Free Press, 1978.

Rosenberg, Bernard, and Norris Fliegel. *The Vanguard Artists: Portrait and Self-Portrait.* Chicago: Quadrangle Books, 1965.

Rosenberg, Harold. *The Anxious Object: Art Today and Its Audience.* New York: Horizon Press, 1964.

Rostow, W. W. *The Stages of Economic Growth.* Cambridge: The University Press, 1963.

Salins, Peter D. *The Ecology of Housing Destruction: Economic Effects of Public Intervention in the Housing Market.* New York: New York University Press, 1980.

———. "The Limits of Gentrification." *New York Affairs* 5, no. 4 (1979): 3–12.

Sandler, Irving. *The Triumph of American Painting: A History of Abstract Expressionism.* New York: Harper & Row Publishers, 1970.

Sayre, Wallace S., and Herbert Kaufman. *Governing New York City.* New York: Russell Sage Foundation, 1960.

Secundus, Junius [pseud.]. "The SoHoiad: or The Masque of Art: A Satire of Heroic Couplets." *New York Review of Books,* March 29, 1984: 17–19.

Seiberling, Dorothy. "SoHo: The Most Exciting Place to Live in the City." *New York Magazine,* May 1974: 52–53.

Siegfried, Alanna, and Helene Zucker Seeman. *SoHo.* New York: Neal-Schuman Publishers, 1978.

Simpson, Charles R. *SoHo: The Artist in the City.* Chicago: University of Chicago Press, 1981.

Smith, Desmond. "Info-City." *New York,* February 9, 1981: 24–29.

SoHo Newsletter, no. 30, October 19, 1972.

SoHo Newsletter, no. 31, January 13, 1973.

SoHo/NoHo: Occupancy Survey (1983). New York City: Department of City Planning, 1985.

SoHo Survey. SoHo Alliance, 1983.

Stratton, Jim. *Pioneering in the Urban Wilderness*. New York: Urizen Books, 1977.

Sumka, Howard J. "Displacement in Revitalizing Neighborhoods: A Review and Research Strategy." Occasional Papers in Housing and Community Affairs. Washington, D.C.: Department of Housing and Urban Development, 1978.

Suttles, Gerald D. "The Cumulative Texture of Local Urban Culture." *American Journal of Sociology* 90, no. 2 (September 1984): 283–304.

————. *The Social Order of the Slum*. Chicago: University of Chicago Press, 1968.

————. "The Social Uses of Community: Interactional, Sentimental and Organizational Elements in the Construction of Communities." Paper presented at the 1979 Annual Meetings of the American Sociological Association.

Taylor, Angela. "A Loft That Looks Lived In." *New York Times*, November 3, 1977: C–8.

Theodorson, George A., ed. *Urban Patterns: Studies in Human Ecology*. Rev. ed. University Park: Pennsylvania State University Press, 1982.

Tobier, Emanuel. "Setting the Record Straight on Loft Conversions." *New York Affairs* 6, no. 4 (1981): 33–44.

Toll, Seymour I. *Zoned American*. New York: Grossman Publishers, 1969.

Tomkins, Calvin. *Off the Wall: Robert Rauschenberg and the Art World of Our Time*. Garden City, N.Y.: Doubleday & Co., 1980.

Urban Affairs Quarterly. Special issue: "The Revitalization of Inner-City Neighborhoods." Vol. 15, no. 4 (June 1980).

Van Liere, Kent D. "Ecological Succession and Community Development." Paper presented at the Annual Meetings of the American Sociological Association, August 1977.

Van Til, Jon. "Citizen Participation in Neighborhood Transformation: A Social Movement Approach." *Urban Affairs Quarterly* 15, no. 4 (June 1980): 439–52.

Wallace, McHarg, Roberts, and Todd. The Lower Manhattan Plan; capital project ES–1. [By] Wallace, McHarg, Roberts and Todd, Whittlesey, Conklin and Rossant [and] Alan M. Voorhees and Associates, Inc. Prepared for the New York City Planning Commission. New York, 1966.

Ware, Caroline. *Greenwich Village 1920–1930: A Comment on American Civilization in the Post-War Years*. New York: Harper & Row, 1965.

Weisbrod, Carl. "Loft Conversion: Will Enforcement Bring Acceptance?" *New York Affairs* 6, no. 4 (1981): 45–56.

Wilkie Farr & Gallagher. *Housing for Artists: The New York Experience.* Prepared for Volunteer Lawyers for the Arts. 1976.

Wiseman, Carter. "The Next Great Place: The Triumph of Battery Park City." *New York Magazine,* June 16, 1986: 34–41.

Whalen, Richard J. "A City Destroying Itself." *Fortune* 70, no. 3 (September 1964): 115 ff.

Willhelm, Sidney M. "The Concept of the 'Ecological Complex': A Critique." *American Journal of Economics and Sociology* 23, no. 3 (1962): 242–48.

———. *Urban Zoning and Land-Use Theory.* New York: The Free Press, 1962.

Winkleman, Michael. "The New Frontier: Housing for the Artist-Industrial." *New York Affairs* 5, no. 4 (1978): 49–57.

Wolfe, Tom. *From Bauhaus to Our House.* New York: Farrar, Straus and Giroux, 1981.

Zeitz, Eileen. *Private Urban Renewal: A Different Residential Trend.* Lexington, Mass.: D. C. Heath & Co., 1979.

Zimmer, Basil G., and Amos H. Hawley. *Metropolitan Area Schools: Resistance to District Reorganization.* Beverly Hills, Calif.: Sage Publications, 1968.

Zimmer, William. "Still Funky But Oh So Chic SoHo." *Art News,* November 1980: 91–93.

Zoning Handbook: A Guide to New York City Zoning Resolution, 4th ed. New York City: Department of City Planning, 1980.

Zukin, Sharon. *Loft Living: Culture and Capital in Urban Change.* Baltimore: Johns Hopkins University Press, 1982.

Index